The Art of
Handbell Ringing

The Art of
Handbell Ringing

NANCY POORE TUFTS

ABINGDON PRESS

New York
Nashville

THE ART OF HANDBELL RINGING

Copyright © 1961 by Abingdon Press

Library of Congress Catalog Card Number: 60-16924

SET UP, PRINTED, AND BOUND BY THE
PARTHENON PRESS, AT NASHVILLE,
TENNESSEE, UNITED STATES OF AMERICA

To my husband,

who for long has heard the bell with me
and
shared in its happy associations,

*this small volume is, with all affection,
inscribed*

Preface

THIS MANUAL IS AN AMPLIFICATION OF A SERIES OF MY contributions entitled "Tintinnabulations," which appeared in *Choristers Guild Letters,* the late Ruth Krehbiel Jacobs, editor, from 1956-60; of similar articles published in *Music Ministry* and other periodicals; and of material used at handbell workshops conducted in various parts of the United States. It is an attempt to answer the hundreds of inquiries about handbell ringing that continually crowd my desk.

I have endeavored to set down, in a practical and brief manner, what I have learned and what I might suggest as a result of experimentation with handbell bands and choirs, of both adults and children, who have discovered along with me the satisfaction and joy of ringing.

Ringingly yours!
—NANCY POORE TUFTS

Acknowledgments

I am happy to have this opportunity to express my appreciation and thanks to all those who have encouraged and helped me, directly or indirectly, to accomplish this manual.

Firstly, I wish to send up a grateful prayer of thanks to the late Margaret H. Shurcliff, "First Lady Bell Ringer of America," and to the late Ruth Krehbiel Jacobs for planting seeds of inspiration and nurturing their growth with kindly interest and enthusiasm; secondly, I wish to express my deep appreciation and humble thanks to three eminent campanologists who have reviewed and corrected this manual—Mr. A. A. Hughes of the Whitechapel Bell Foundry of London, Frederick Sharpe ("Mr. F♯"), President of the Central Council of Church Bell Ringers of England, and Scott Parry, author of *The Story of Handbells;* special thanks also to Mrs. Lillian D. Meyers, who corrected and typed the manuscript; thanks to American bell leaders—James R. Lawson, Norma Lowder, Florence Marlow, Wendell Westcott, and F. L. Whittlesey—and English experts, Norman Chaddock and the Rev. F. F. Rigby for their advice and encouragement; thanks to Arthur Leslie Jacobs and Kathryn Hill Rawls, to Mildred Gleeson and Cornelia Kinsella for their loyalty and interest, and to the Rev. Joseph Tatnall, who graciously permitted me to experiment for four years with the use of handbell music in services of worship; lastly, to thank the hundreds of handbell ringers who have served as unsuspecting guinea pigs—particularly charter members of the Potomac English Handbell Ringers—Della Bruce Currier, Howard Griffith, Jessie Draffin Griffith, William O. Tufts, and Lydia Wells.

N. P. T.

Contents

Chapter I

A Brief History of Handbells

AN AMERICAN PHENOMENON OF THE 1950's WAS THE amazing and enthusiastic growth of the "ancient and honorable art of English handbell ringing" throughout the United States. Introduced in Boston by the late Margaret Shurcliff, who organized the Beacon Hill Ringers *ca.* 1925, this delightful musical activity simmered in the New England area for several decades, then by the middle of the century began to catch fire and spread rapidly across the country.

Music directors have embraced handbell ringing as a unique and worthy contribution to the musical program of schools, churches, and community organizations. Handbell ringing has also been welcomed as a hobby, particularly by "golden age" groups, by the blind, and by therapists for use in mental institutions.

The sound of a bell has appealed inexplicably to the hearts of mankind throughout the ages; traditions and associations connected with bell ringing are intricately woven through the fabric of Western culture. The lore of bells is virtually endless.

The origin of bells is lost forever in the earliest beginnings of history. The first crude bells fashioned of clay or wood by primitive man were certainly handbells. Rough handgrips of leather thongs or wood were attached and the bells were rung by hand, or suspended in trees and tapped with sticks, or hung around the necks of grazing animals. Such bells inevitably played an integral part in various festivities and religious ceremonials. The ringing of bells has ever held a deep religious significance, a mystique, for peoples of all ages and cultures.

Although references to bells exist on Egyptian monuments, in the writings of the Greek philosophers, in Chinese literature, and in the Old Testament, there was no authoritative information before the Christian Era. Handbells were used to call the early Christians to worship. The usage of the Latin words *campana* and *nola* to denote "large bell in a tower" and "small bell" have led some authorities to credit Paulinus, a Bishop of Nola, in Campania, Italy, *ca.* 400, with having been the first to introduce bells into the Christian church. At any rate, towers built to house larger bells have come to be known as campaniles, and the term for the science of bell ringing, campanology. Sabinianus, who was Pope *ca.* 600, first gave the sanction of the church to the use of bells and decreed that bells should be rung to announce hours of worship.

As Christianity fanned out from Italy, missionaries tramped purposefully over mountains and through marshes spreading the glad tidings of redemption and ringing small handbells to summon the people together. Churches and bell towers appeared in their wake throughout the

12

Continent and westward to the British Isles. At first, bell towers were built apart from the church, but later they were added on to the church structure itself. Bells have had a remarkable influence on architecture; and it is probably due to them that we owe many of the great towers of the world.

While the carillon developed in the Low Countries from watchtowers containing a single bell to "singing towers" housing from twenty-one to seventy-two or more bells, allowing a wide range for tunes and harmonies, the English preferred a "ring of bells." Few English belfries house more than a dozen bells, the average being six to eight, which are swung by teams of men and women vigorously pulling ropes by hand. "Change ringing" is based on mathematical rather than musical principles, and while there is no melody or harmony to charm the ear and titillate the senses, the sheer weight of sound piled up by these giant bells is a never-to-be-forgotten thrill.

Handbells as we know them today were devised in the sixteenth and seventeenth centuries by English tower bell ringers as a means of practicing change ringing. It was much more comfortable to sit around a table in a heated choir room—or at the local tavern—and practice with small bells having leather or wooden handgrips than to spend tiresome hours in a cold tower swinging heavy bells with ropes. Some peals require several hours to complete. Long periods of bell practice may become a public nuisance.

By 1700, larger sets of handbells were being cast by bell foundries and "tune ringing" became popular. The custom developed in certain localities for handbell ringers, like carolers or waits, to appear in the streets, on the village greens, or on church steps and ring carols, hymns, and folk songs on festal occasions such as Christmastide, May Day, and Harvest Home. By the early nineteenth century, tune ringing flourished in its heyday. Ringing bands of Lancashire, Yorkshire, and Cheshire reportedly employing two hundred bells and playing from symphonic scores, gave concerts and competed in exciting contests.

Many single tower bells, the "Liberty Bell," and several "rings of bells" were shipped to the American colonies from the "Ringing Isles" during the eighteenth century. Paul Revere of Boston cast thirty-seven single church bells. American historians, as yet, have been unable to find any reference to handbells in the Colonies, although this custom was undoubtedly known to colonists of English background and to those visiting England during that period. Tom Ingram in *Bells in England* mentions that Benjamin Franklin exercised on a dumbbell machine, a contraption of ropes and weights, invented for the use of tower bell ringers.

The first reference to handbells in the United States, so far uncovered, was in the early 1840's when P. T. Barnum, America's great showman, heard a prize tune-ringing band —the "Lancashire Ringers"—in Liverpool and engaged them for an American tour. Barnum decided to glamorize these Englishmen by dressing them in colorful Swiss costumes, and billed them as "Swiss Bell Ringers," a misnomer which has unfortunately clung to English handbells in this country. While it is thought that Barnum's "Swiss Bell

Ringers" were the first to be heard in America, the Peake family of ringers was known to have toured the East in the same decade, and may have antedated Barnum. However, Barnum's ringers visited the tower of Christ Church, Philadelphia, while in this country, and were the first to accomplish a complete peal in America.

During the latter half of the nineteenth century handbell ringing in America consisted almost entirely of a few ringers in vaudeville, and later in Chautauqua. Most of the bells used were of inferior quality and were coated with silver or nickel to enhance their show appearance.

Around the turn of the present century, Arthur Nichols introduced handbells in the New England area for practice by the tower bell ringers of Old North Church and of Groton School. In 1923 his daughter, Mrs. Arthur Shurcliff of Boston, organized a tune ringing band, the Beacon Hill Ringers, a group which is still ringing every Christmas Eve on Beacon Hill for thousands of happy "live" listeners, as well as for radio and television audiences. In 1954, the American Guild of English Handbell Ringers was chartered at Castle Hill, Ipswich, Massachussetts. Today the guild has a membership of approximately two hundred bands and one hundred individuals, a total of over 1,500 ringing members. There are many other groups in existence and new ones springing up every few days. The two major foundries manufacturing handbells are swamped with orders from America.

Although numerous bell-ringing customs still prevail in the "Ringing Isles," where change ringing is still actively practiced, interest in tune ringing has waned; and many bands have disappeared. The discovery of the joy of hand-bell ringing by Americans, and its mushrooming popularity with musicians and audiences, is a modern renaissance of an ancient folk art that attained a high peak of perfection in the early nineteenth century.

Handbell ringing is proving a joy and delight to ringer and listener alike, whether an ensemble of professional caliber ringing classical selections in many parts, or a group of youngsters or hobbyists ringing simple melodies with a dozen bells.

Chapter II

General Description of Handbells

GOOD HANDBELLS ARE CAST OF "BELL METAL," AN ALLOY of copper and tin, the proportion being approximately 80 per cent to 20 per cent. Handbells do not have the minor, plaintive quality characteristic of carillon bells, but they have a predominant twelfth overtone. This is a distinct advantage in harmonic effects and in ensemble playing with choral groups, organ, piano, and with solo instruments. Unless otherwise requested handbells are tuned to standard pitch—A-440.

Modern handbells are fitted with handles or handgrips made of leather straps, which allow the ringer dynamic control. The pitch name is stamped on both sides of the handles. Clappers are detachable for replacement or repair. So that the metal ball of the clapper may never come in contact with the metal of the bell proper (sound bow), clapper balls are tipped with leather or wooden pegs. The ball and pegs of larger clappers are covered with felt strips. Two springs are attached to the staple and serve as a brake for the clapper shaft to prevent it from swinging uncontrollably, as a dinner-bell clapper. Each spring has a piece of felt glued on the inner surface at the point of contact with the clapper shaft. Again, metal does not touch metal.

The total number of handbells manufactured is five complete chromatic octaves, sixty-one bells, ranging in sound from C below middle C to two octaves above high C. (Exception: The Whitechapel Foundry is equipped to produce a sixth octave of tiny bells.) However, for convenience in writing, handbells are considered a transposing instrument of one octave. Hereinafter in this manual all pitches referred to are transposed (writing) pitch, actually sounding one octave higher. Like the music for the bass viol, handbell music is written one octave lower than actual sound. This is important to remember in ordering handbells, especially as the larger

Diagram 1

Handbells are considered as a transposing instrument. The actual sound is one octave higher than written.

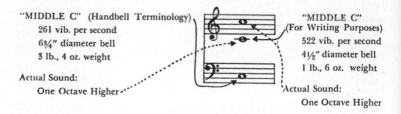

"MIDDLE C" (Handbell Terminology)
    261 vib. per second
    6¾" diameter bell
    3 lb., 4 oz. weight

Actual Sound:
    One Octave Higher

"MIDDLE C"
(For Writing Purposes)
    522 vib. per second
    4½" diameter bell
    1 lb., 6 oz. weight

Actual Sound:
    One Octave Higher

bells are much more expensive and may be too heavy for young persons and small-wristed women to handle. The heaviest handbell manufactured weighs approximately ten pounds; the lightest, four ounces. Considering a practical set of, say, two octaves, from G below middle C on up, the heaviest bell would weigh about two pounds and the lightest, nine ounces.

What Comprises a Set?

It is not necessary to order a prescribed number of bells. Directors may order any number or combination they wish or can afford—from one to sixty-one! There is no financial advantage in ordering "sets." However, one foundry makes an additional charge of 10 per cent for orders of less than twelve bells. Unless one expects to ring only simple melodic lines, perhaps with younger children, or desires a small ring solely for the practice of change ringing, the purchase of fewer than fifteen bells is not recommended. The harmonic effects produced by handbells can be indescribably beautiful. Why settle for less?

Directors order various numbers of bells according to their budget, needs, and individual preferences. In general, except for those few who own five chromatic octaves of bells (sixty-one), the total number available, "sets" tend to fall into three categories: (1) fourteen to eighteen bells, or approximately one and one-half diatonic octaves ranging from middle C to G above the treble staff, plus several sharps; (2) twenty-five bells, two full chromatic octaves, ranging from G below middle C to G above the treble staff; (3) thirty-seven bells, three full chromatic octaves, ranging from C, the octave below middle C, to C, two octaves above middle C. Many successful directors gradually add bells to their sets—perhaps a bass bell or two, or a missing sharp. Larger set owners might keep in mind how little a bass C-sharp, D-sharp will be used, and how many small bells could be purchased for the price of one big "bucket."

Sets of three or more octaves are most satisfactory, musically, and are a joy to the music arranger in that carols, hymns, and folk songs, by judicious juggling, may be played almost as written. A large number of bells also present more problems to the director—recruitment, assignment and arrangement of bells, absences (substitutes), transportation, storage and care of bells—to name a few.

A two-to-three-octave set is perhaps the most satisfactory to handle with the average group of teen-agers and adults. Many interesting and effective harmonic and polyphonic musical compositions may be arranged and composed within this range. Here are enough larger, sonorous bells to challenge the mighty male muscle—yet not too heavy for an active girl or woman to handle—plus a number of smaller, clear-toned bells that can soar over and above other instruments and congregational singing, and yet can achieve silvery pianissimos.

A small, fifteen-bell set is not to be scorned. This weight set would be especially satisfactory for fifth, sixth, and seventh graders, for small teen-agers, and ladies' groups. With this number of bells, two or three-voice treble arrangements of hymns, carols, and folk songs may be written acceptably in the keys of C, G, and F, and change ringing may be practiced. Ingenious directors have devised many charming, artistic, and even thrilling effects

20

with a small ring of bells. Mrs. Lloyd Runkle, director of the ringers of Cape Ann, Gloucester, Massachusetts, who has pioneered in bell ringing with high-school girls, achieves outstanding results with a thirteen-bell set. The Berkshire Ringers of Pittsfield, Massachusetts, Mrs. David Caird, director, who ring in a singularly beautiful manner, have a sixteen-bell set.

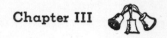

Chapter III

The Organization of Handbell Groups

Our Music's so sweet, so enchanting to hear
We wish there was Ringing each day in the year
—Anonymous

Types of Ringing Groups

MUSIC TEACHERS, CHOIR DIRECTORS, AND OTHER LEADERS who work with groups of young people or adults will usually find that the organization of a handbell band or choir will be a problem of elimination rather than of formation. When the handbells are unpacked and their clear tones reverberate through the halls, the line will form on the right. The director will be a Pied Piper, and his popularity rating will zoom to astronomical heights. Seriously, this author has never known any musical phenomenon to attract and hold the attention of young people, especially, as does handbell ringing.

Handbell Choirs

The largest number of handbell groups are connected with the music programs of churches and are called bell choirs. Choir directors are using handbells with all age groups to beautify and augment the music in services of worship. Although the majority of such choirs are composed of youngsters of junior and senior high-school age, there are ladies' and men's bell choirs, or mixed groups. Membership in the bell choir may be a reward for superior junior and youth choir achievement, or it may be limited to boys with changing voices, all girls, etc. Here is a golden opportunity to use a group of children with deformities, real monotones and the blind; they, too, can make a joyful noise unto the Lord. Bell ringing has remarkably improved the co-ordination and attention span of many a gangling "bull-in-the-china-shop" teenster. The loyalty and enthusiasm engendered by bell ringing is remarkable. Outstanding bell choirs in this country include: The Ringers of the Village Lutheran Church, Bronxville, New York, Doris Voester, director; The First Congregational Church Ringers, Battle Creek, Michigan, Dr. Robert Heiber, director; The Cathedral Bell Ringers, Atlanta, Georgia, Mrs. Homer Edwards, director; The Pilgrim Ringers of the First Congregational Church of Columbus, Ohio, Edward Johe, director; Ringers of the First Presbyterian Church, Staten Island, New York, and bell choirs of other churches directed by Dr. Doris Watson; and numerous splendid groups throughout America.

Handbell Bands in Schools and Colleges

Music instructors in elementary and secondary schools and in colleges and universities are beginning to realize the value and importance of handbell ringing. School

23

handbell bands and choirs have sprung up in many states. Repertoires vary from the classical to the popular and stunt-type music. Representative school groups are: The Whitechapel Bell Choir of the Atchison High School, Kansas, Joyce Wentz, director; the Handbell Club of the Bryn Mawr School, Baltimore, Maryland, Elizabeth Merriam, director; Mackenzie High School Bells of Detroit, Michigan, Robert F. Delaney, director. Well-known university bands are: The Spartan Ringers of Michigan State University, Dr. Wendell Westcott, director; and Ringing Bands of Princeton University, The University of Chicago, and Bennington College, Vermont.

Here may lie the future of the best bell-ringing techniques in America. With an unlimited choice of personnel the school or college bell director may select the cream of the crop—young people who are already talented, expert musicians. The results can be professional precision and polish, with scores memorized, first-class equipment, and concert opportunities far beyond the possibilities of most church-sponsored groups. However, church and school groups may complement each other, each feeding the other. This will be an interesting development to watch over the next several decades.

Handbell Ringing as a Hobby

Handbell ringing is providing great fun as recreation and as a hobby. A number of groups, especially among housewives and retired persons, are meeting socially to explore the delights of making beautiful sounds together without too much effort or study. The bells are usually privately owned. Perhaps every other person in the world is a thwarted musician at heart. Either he had no opportunity to learn to play a musical instrument, or he had no "talent," or he failed to apply himself. (It was most probably the last reason.) In handbell ringing the thwarted music lover finds a welcome release, for here is an unusual and charming instrument that he can learn to operate passably with only a few, pleasant rehearsals; and thus he can satisfy that inner desire of a lifetime.

"Golden-age" groups in churches, recreational centers, and "homes" find a mild amount of handbell ringing enjoyable and exciting. A worthy project for ringing bands and choirs would be to donate an occasional hour for a visit and a bell jamboree with a group of oldsters. Attention, bell directors!

Community Handbell Ringing Groups

Hobby ringing groups often develop into community and semiprofessional Bands. A congenial group that has rehearsed at length under a capable director and has access to good music arrangements for handbells will undoubtedly become "resident artists" and an asset to the musical life of the community. Public performances soon refine and polish repertoire, stage presence, timing, and whet the ringers' appetites for further ringing adventure.

Community groups range from bands made up of private individuals to bands connected with a local recreational department, civic group, club, or business firm. On the youth level, such bands may represent recreational de-

25

partments, boys' clubs, scouts, Campfire Girls, civic organizations, to name a few. Community ringing bands invariably wear attractive outfits or costumes. Such bands of note are: the famous Beacon Hill Ringers of Boston, Massachusetts, organized by the late Margaret Shurcliff; The Blue Bells of Webster Groves, Missouri, the first band in the Midwest, organized by Florence Marlow; The Quincy Bell Ringers of the Granite Trust Company, Quincy, Massachusetts, directed by Isabel Meldrum; The Paul Revere Ringers of Bedford, Massachusetts, Edna Comrie, director; The Potomac English Handbell Ringers of Washington, D. C., directed by Nancy Poore Tufts; The Regina Rotary Handbell Ringers, Regina, Saskatchewan, Canada, Norman Langdale, conductor.

Ringing Bands for the Blind

Handbell ringing is a delightful and successful hobby for the blind. Two schools—the Perkins Institute for the Blind, Watertown, Masachusetts, and the Overbrook School for the Blind, Philadelphia, Pennsylvania—own sets and have active ringing bands. Several sighted bands include blind members.

Teachers of the blind and music therapists working with the mentally ill have different approaches to organization and training that will not be discussed here.

The Use of Handbells in Music Therapy for the Mentally Ill

Superintendents of several institutions for the mentally ill have expressed approval of handbell ringing as a therapeutic tool. Patients benefit from the feeling of satisfaction in accomplishment, make encouraging group adjustments, and even the very regressed have shown unusual interest in bells and some ability to concentrate on bell music.

Selection of Handbell Ringers

If the number of applicants is large tryouts are in order. Group tryouts are preferable and timesaving.

The selection of ringers should be on the basis of: (1) good rhythm and co-ordination; (2) the ability to read music; (3) strong wrists; (4) alertness and determination; (5) pleasant personality and co-operative attitude; (6) schedule of activities (free time available).

After a brief period of instruction the director can determine (1) and (2) by having candidates ring scale and arpeggio passages, a melody, and a simple harmonization, which have been especially written out on sheets, charts, or blackboard, as test pieces. Candidates might first handle only one bell, progressing to two as proof of good co-ordination.

Strength of wrists, alertness, and determination can all be ascertained during this period. Prospects might exchange bells so that the director may decide which are best suited to individual ringers. Although some proficient ringers have made a weak show of strength in the beginning, ordinarily those who acquire the knack almost immediately will undoubtedly prove to be fast learners and strong players. An occasional applicant, usually a heavy-armed male, will overring, creating a harsh, undesirable

27

tone which he may always have trouble controlling. Such persons should be accepted with caution.

If further eliminations are necessary, applicants might be tested handling more than two bells, that is, changing bells, during one composition. In the event that new ringers are being selected as regular or substitute members for an experienced group, the group itself might vote on the most promising prospects. It would be wise, in many cases, to set up a second-string and even third-string choir or band, perhaps of younger age, using a smaller ring of bells to give more persons the opportunity of learning to ring, to provide substitutes, and to feed the membership of the number one group. These other groups might be started after the first group has achieved a measure of success and popularity and everybody yearns to climb on the band wagon.

If the number of applicants to be considered is small perhaps (1), (5), and (6) must be the only requisites for membership. In many small, volunteer groups, it is sometimes expedient to accept Mary in order to have Martha, or Mrs. Smith in order to snare Mr. Smith.

Assignment of Handbells

It is difficult to make arbitrary rules about handbell ringing because there is no final authority except for the rules governing change ringing, which are of little concern or help to the music director. Even the English tune-ringing Bands, with their historic backgrounds, differ among themselves concerning various practices and techniques. Music is jealously guarded. American directors, with little information available, have more or less pioneered as to handbell ringing techniques and have experimented by trial and error. Each group has its own peculiar problems, and there are many solutions.

Handbells are assigned to ringers by a number of systems. Assignment depends on the number of ringers available; their size, age, and strength; the size and weight of the bells to be used; the type of music to be played; the positions of players in formation or at a table.

Many directors assign bells to ringers in scale-wise progression, others in octaves (one player ringing C and its octave, the next player ringing D and its octave, etc.), and some in other ways.

Here is a suggested assignment for a fifteen-bell set, using seven ringers:

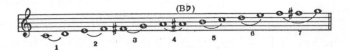

Diagram 2

Directors with many prospective ringers might at first be tempted to use twelve or fifteen Ringers with a fifteen-bell set. However, ringers handling only one bell or a bell that rings only occasionally become bored and lose interest. It is better to use as few ringers as possible and keep them busy.

Here is a suggested assignment for a two chromatic octave set, using ten ringers:

Diagram 3

Fully chromatic sets complicate bell assignments. Ringers must help one another and be alert. Each ringer should have a small loose-leaf notebook marked with his name and position number, a page for each musical selection in the repertoire, and an index of selections. On each page he lists what bells he rings in the work listed on that page so that he may refer to it quickly at rehearsals and concerts. Such a notebook serves as a guide for substitutes. During programs and religious services it is less conspicuous and more convenient that each ringer have a specially prepared single sheet or card with the necessary information.

Referring to Diagram 2, therefore, in a selection written in the key of D, Ringers 3 and 7 may help Ringer 10 with a C-sharp. Ringer 10 may, in turn, be helping another ringer with an inconvenient accidental. It is usually more practical for ringers to help the nearest ringer in order to avoid passing bells any distance, although this passing can be worked out if thoroughly understood and practiced by all concerned. (Having access to a duplicate set of bells is most helpful to the solution of this problem.) Ringer 10, by the way, is a "roving" ringer, who though assigned certain sharps, is generally more free to help than others. A roving ringer should be a most experienced and alert ringer. A new ringer should be assigned a stationary position.

If more than ten ringers are used with a two-octave set several ringers will not play often. Bell music is usually written in the simpler keys of C, G, D, F, and B-flat. In the key of G, F-natural may not play; in the key of D, neither F-natural nor C-natural may play much; and similarly speaking, many bells will not sound in each composition. Interest must be maintained with ringers. A bored ringer is a liability.

Here is a suggested assignment for a three-octave set, using twelve ringers:

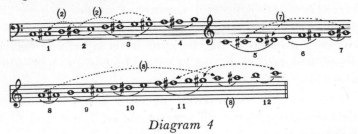

Diagram 4

Twelve ringers can handle three chromatic octaves of handbells nicely, especially when tables are used. Ringer 2 may help ringer 1 with C-sharp and ringer 3 with any bell; ringer 7 may help ringer 5 with C-sharp and D-sharp. Ringer 8 is responsible for A and A-sharp and also for A and A-sharp an octave higher. Ringer 12 may help 11 and 8, or other ringers. The highest bells are usually not required often enough to warrant a thirteenth ringer. Generally ringers handling bells in the middle range are busier than those handling the high and low ranges.

Bell directors having sets of more than three chromatic octaves to work with may find bell assignments increasingly difficult. The more bells to handle, the more problems to face. As stated in a preceding paragraph, the main concern is to keep additional ringers busy, that is, happy. Actually, this author uses only twelve ringers for a five-octave set, plus a duplicate three-octave set. Fourteen or fifteen ringers could be kept reasonably busy; however, again those ringing the lowest and highest bells may sit out several numbers.

Twelve quick-on-the-trigger ringers, handling a five-octave set, might be assigned in the same fashion as for the three-octave set. Ringers 1 through 4 would each be responsible for the same lettered bells an octave lower; Ringers 9 through 12 for the same lettered bells an octave higher. Ringers 2, 7, 8, and 12 might be freest to help with extra bells.

Regardless of the number of bells and the number of ringers, the director can save untold confusion and time by designating the bells in each selection for each ringer. He may write these directions in each individual notebook or prepare a sheet or card for each ringer, to be given the ringer as new pieces are rehearsed. The ringer may copy this information in a notebook or maintain a file or collection of cards or sheets. Ideally, the director himself should prepare a master notebook for reference. Directors arranging assignments for large sets of bells may find it a jigsaw puzzle at first, but time and experience will ease the burden.

Position Assignment

Individual directors will have different ideas and reasons for lining up a ringing ensemble as to exact location of each ringer. Those assigning bells in scale-wise progression may arrange the group in a single line or semi-circle, the lower bells on the left, the higher on the right, or vice versa. Those using a double, staggered line may have a similar arrangement with variations. Perhaps height or sex will determine the final location. Undoubtedly, a group makes a better appearance when the tallest are centered, the shortest at opposite ends.

Ringers using tables must also be given permanent ringing positions. This may be governed by the size and number of tables, bells, and ringers. Although having the largest bells centered on a table makes for a balanced picture, this may upset a scale-wise assignment. This matter is up to the director's judgment and taste.

Conclusion

Because bell ringers are human the above suggestions are far from foolproof. Each group has one or more "eager beavers" who "champ at the bit" for higher hurdles to conquer and who are challenged by the opportunity of handling bells in quantity. On the other hand, there are cautious souls who "freeze" to two or three bells and unwillingly share, experiment, or change.

And so the perceptive director must also work out assignments according to personalities, ability, and alertness. Personality and co-operative attitude are perhaps the most important ingredients of a successful handbell organization.

Chapter IV

How to Ring Handbells, or the Quest for Bellmanship

THERE IS LITTLE MYSTERY ABOUT RINGING A HANDBELL. THE knack is easy to acquire. After a few preliminary rehearsals the technique is unconsciously assumed by the average ringer, and following rehearsals may be devoted to learning notes and perfecting the ensemble.

Fundamental Procedure

Bell ringing does not involve a long process of technical development comparable to that required of students of some musical instruments. At the first rehearsal prospective ringers must be instructed in the proper way to hold a bell. Bells are grasped firmly by the leather straps as near the leather cap (circle) as possible. The hand is closed in fistlike position around the handle with the thumb either on top of the other fingers or resting against the edge of the leather cap but not touching the metal. The bell is held upright, slanted slightly inward toward the chest—which tilts the clapper back, ready to strike. A quick forward and downward stroke of the wrist, stopping

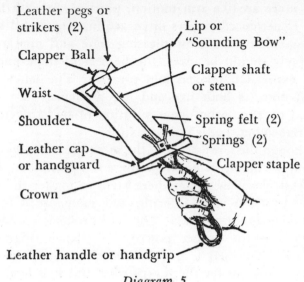

Leather pegs or strikers (2)

Lip or "Sounding Bow"

Clapper Ball

Clapper shaft or stem

Waist

Shoulder

Spring felt (2)

Springs (2)

Leather cap or handguard

Clapper staple

Crown

Leather handle or handgrip

Diagram 5

horizontally in front of the body, produces a firm ring. The ringer should practice this stroke in each hand until it becomes natural, then tackle ringing two bells alternately. Next, the group might essay a scale or peal exercise; then a familiar melody or two; and, lastly, a simple harmonization of a familiar carol or hymn. Although there are directors who drill ringers in many scales, arpeggios, and other exercises, the average group has limited time for rehearsal, and save for brief warm-up exercises, this time is best spent learning music.

After a firm stroke is established new ringers should be advised not to "hug" the bells but gradually to practice a freer, more arc-like arm motion, particularly with larger bells. Experienced ringers often acquire a graceful swing that makes for the most pleasing tone and appearance. The body should be erect, the head held high, and the facial expression relaxed and pleasant. The latter is of special note, as both live and TV audiences have commented on the "grim" concentration of bell ringers. Always remember, bell ringing is fun!

Although the downstroke is the more generally accepted method of ringing in America, there is a possible upstroke or backstroke. Few ringers here seem to master the backstroke, which is more difficult, and some use it mainly for ringing repeated notes. The backstroke is a necessary position for the proper practice of change ringing on handbells. The bell is grasped in the same manner for the backstroke as for the downstroke, but it is held horizontally instead of upright and is moved toward the shoulder by a quick, upward motion of the wrist. The backstroke is checked by the thumb which is placed smartly against the leather cap as the bell swings up. Many English bands employ the backstroke almost exclusively, chiefly those who use small diatonic change ringing sets. The Norbury Ringers of Stockport and the Ecclesfield Ringers of Sheffield are foremost exponents of this method with large sets of bells. However, Frederick Sharpe, English campanologist and historian, claims that the "traditional" English method is the four-in-hand described on page 40. There is little unanimity about tune-ringing techniques or methods of writing music among the English ringers. These differences of opinion have been the subject of much discussion in *The Ringing World* for years. While the backstroke can be useful, it is not likely that the four-in-hand method will become popular in America where the supply of ringers seems inexhaustible.

Control of Dynamics

Ringers can soon learn to control their strokes and to ring *piano, mezzo forte,* and *forte* when this is frequently called to their attention by the director. Too many bands and choirs are allowed to ring "full voice" at all times and must depend on the variety of music programed for contrast rather than using dynamic variation. Other ringing directors exploit the tiny tone, the fairy-bell effect; and while beautiful and ethereal, this too becomes monotonous.

Dampening or Muting

Dampening is a matter of the individual preference or taste of the director. A fundamental characteristic of all swinging bells is free reverberation. It is a moot question among bell directors whether to tamper with resonating bells by terminating the sound abruptly or to allow the sound to die naturally.

Those advocating a minimum of dampening employ it for special staccato effects such as in "The Grandfather's Clock" and "The Lass with the Delicate Air," to imitate a harp or harpsichord, to mute quickly following a performance during a religious service, a radio or TV program, or to dampen an occasional predominating large bell. Dampening with precision requires much rehearsal.

Dampening is most effectively accompanied by merely

holding the bell against the chest or arm or padded table. Care should be taken to avoid hitting bells against buttons, jewelry, and hard objects. Bells may also be muted by touching the lip with the thumb, small bells by moving the thumb onto the metal nearest the leather cap. However, it is well to establish the rule about never touching metal with the hands, as perspiration dulls the polish and fingerprints are unsightly.

Bell choirs or bands employing larger bells may find it advisable to dampen bass bells during chromatic passages or sudden changes of harmony. The beat of the largest bells manufactured, particularly, is sometimes disturbing. The bell-music arranger should remember these problems.

Ringers who have made recordings of their playing have heard in exaggeration the overhang of certain predominating bells. Such a recording would well serve as a guide to those who wish to carry the practice of dampening further, and as a warning to the music arranger.

Suffice it to say that frequent dampening, when well done, requires much practice and is an additional burden to those directors and ringers alike who have limited rehearsal time and full ringing schedules ahead. Some perceptive musicians find the sudden cessation of bell resonance as disturbing as others find its continuance. The overhang is more apparent in live rooms and auditoriums, over a public-address system, and recording equipment.

Tremulando and Trill

The tremulando is employed frequently as a means of sustaining a melody note above No. 12 F (Whitechapel numbering). This device is used by carillonneurs to sustain single notes and chords, but it can be overworked. Excessive ornamentation effects as used by Couperin and other writers for the harpsichord become tedious and precious. Occasional use of a tremulando, such as the climactic phrase of "The Star-Spangled Banner," "Land of the free," and the refrain of the hymn "Rejoice, Ye Pure in Heart" (Marion), "Rejoice, rejoice, rejoice, give thanks and sing," are most successful.

An even tremulando is not difficult to achieve and is effected by simply allowing the clapper to strike back and forth rapidly. A high speed requires considerable practice. The smaller the bell, the easier the tremulando.

The tremulando is not to be confused with the trill, which requires two bells rung by one person. A rapid, even trill is most difficult to accomplish and requires much practice. Many proficient ringers never learn to trill satisfactorily, so the director must arrange bell assignments and passing for those ringers who acquire the knack of trilling with ease. A director of a less-experienced group might utilize the tremulando in place of the trill as an effective and simple substitute.

Swinging

An interesting effect may be obtained on a final chord or special cadence of a selection by swinging the bells just sounded. As soon as the chord is struck, those ringers who played lower their bells and swing them slowly in unison, at arm's length, preferably for two half-circles:

strike, down, back, forward, back, forward, up, position, This pealing effect is especially appropriate following a slow harmonious selection. It should not be overdone—perhaps once in a program. It *is* a stunt.

Novelty Effects

It is not wise to tap bells with sharp sticks or metal objects. Amusing effects may be added to a program with the use of wood blocks, chimney flutes, sleigh (or other) bells, and drums. Every group should have a novelty encore. This, too, can be overdone.

Handbell Carillon and Four-in-Hand Ringing

Ringing groups with insufficient personnel to handle the number of bells available may employ a handbell carillon or rack, or ringers of smaller bells may handle two bells in each hand—four-in-hand ringing.

Handbells may be suspended from a rack similar to a clothes rack with one or more parallel poles and struck with a felt-covered mallet. A number of bells can be rung by an adept player and perhaps one assistant. Comment: The bell tone achieved is not apt to be so full as when rung by hand.

Small adult groups, particularly in England, are accustomed to holding two bells of any size in each hand. The strap handles are held in the hand at right angles to each other, one being looped around the forefinger, the other around the thumb. A safe arrangement is to pass the strap of one bell through the strap of the other and grasp firmly to ring. It is difficult to acquire the wrist snap to produce a firm tone or stroke with two bells in one hand, the clappers being at right angles to each other. One bell is preferable.

Solo Ringing

A popular and enjoyable stunt is solo ringing on handbells. With a fair amount of practice an adept ringer can arrange a number of bells in a certain order on a padded table and ring melodies and even simple harmonies, with excellent effect. A final chord of four bells will bring huzzahs from the audience! A piano, organ, or handbell accompaniment improves the performance. For variety a group of solo numbers included on a program allows a break for the band or choir but more importantly gives the director an opportunity to feature an outstanding ringer or two. The bell director himself might consider attaining a degree of proficiency in solo ringing in order to demonstrate bell-ringing during the inevitable talks and lectures he may be expected to give from time to time.

Handbells in Ensemble

Tuned handbells often blend well in ensemble with solo voices, choruses, solo instruments, groups of instruments, and with other handbells.

Bells may be employed as an accompaniment for solo voices and instruments, choruses, and congregational singing; as a solo ensemble with piano, organ, harp, or orchestral background; for interludes, countermelodies, and descant effects during solos and choruses. Bells blend more successfully with wind and string instruments than with percussive instruments. A list of suggestions of vocal and instrumental material to be used with handbells is included elsewhere in this manual.

Antiphonal Ringing

Ringing bands and choirs using two sets of bells or planning a joint concert with another ringing group will find antiphonal ringing quite exciting. One group may be placed in a gallery or the rear of an auditorium, the other in front; or a group may be situated in another room or in the wings for an echo effect. The German carol, "While by Our Sleeping Flocks We Lay," as rung antiphonally by the bell choirs of Drs. Whittlesey and Barcarfer of Dallas, Texas, was the high light of the Second Southwestern Handbell Festival.

Out-of-Door Ringing

The handbell tone is also beautiful in the out-of-doors, especially when atmospheric conditions are favorable. Bells should be amplified if the sound is expected to carry any distance or to be heard by a large audience. The ringing group should stand preferably on the steps of a building, or in front of a wall, so that the sound may be thrown out.

Ringing in Processionals

Handbells have been used for centuries in processionals. The historic Bayeux tapestry of the eleventh century pictures the funeral procession of Edward the Confessor, which included several bell ringers. Frederick Sharpe, president of the Central Council of Church Bell Ringers of

England, has written that handbells were used at funerals between the eleventh and sixteenth centuries and are still rung in procession on certain ceremonial occasions. An old print of a typical harvest home festival parade or processional, which appears in an English periodical of 1860, shows a team of bell ringers ringing handbells held high above their heads.

This author has never forgotten the thrill of hearing some 150 youthful ringers, marching in dignified procession in a church, ringing a hymn in harmony. The congregation sang with appreciation and fervor. Altogether, it was a most impressive occasion. Similar processionals for a school, patriotic, or community function could be equally effective.

Ringing in processionals should be well rehearsed, or else not attempted. Nothing should be left to chance.

Less-experienced groups can make a worthy contribution by merely ringing a melody, perhaps in octave unisons, or a descant, or even a fanfare or other figuration between verses of a song.

Those groups having no time for memorization may carry music by hand or fasten it to a sleeve.

Needless to say, the band or choir appearance and mien is of paramount importance. Ringers should stand and walk erectly in a stately manner with eyes ahead; spacing and keeping together should be practiced and precise; bells should be held up straight at chest level, or against the chest; robes and costumes should be neat and pressed, bells freshly polished. "Here come the bell ringers!"

43

Handbell Festivals

Handbell festivals, mostly under the aegis of the American Guild of English Handbell Ringers, are now being held more and more throughout the country and provide an unparalleled opportunity for numbers of ringing bands and choirs to appear together and to ring simultaneously.

What could be more thrilling than to play with dozens of ringers handling hundreds of bells? The possibilities of handbell ringing are limited only by the imaginations of the handbell directors.

Chapter V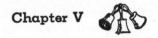

Handbell Equipment

Storage or Carrying Cases

A MAJOR CONCERN OF BELL DIRECTORS IS THE PROTECTION and safety of the bells. All handbell sets should be insured against damage, theft, and loss. Carrying cases, such as the padded metal cases manufactured by Petit & Fritsen, are the safest for storage and transportation. Numerous ringing groups are using ingeniously constructed wooden boxes or cases with partitions and special spaces for individual bells. Each bell is immobilized within its niche by a clamp or strap fastening. Such boxes or cases have tops, locks, and handles for carrying.

Groups with small rings of bells often store and carry the bells in one or two suitcases. Cloth, cotton, or foam rubber should be wrapped between the bells to protect them from knocking against one another. Individual bell bags made of flannel or pacific cloth with the pitch names written or sewn on in a conspicuous place are the most convenient protection.

Several groups having large numbers of bells are using foot lockers lined and layered with foam rubber. This

45

author knows of no cases made commercially for the largest bells. Each carrying case, box, or locker should be equipped with several soft flannel or other metal-polishing cloths.

Tables

Ringing groups using tables will find it practical to own one or more. An excellent buy is a 72″ x 33″ aluminum folding table. These tables are easily set up, can be stored in a closet or against the wall, and are conveniently packed or carried on trips.

Robert Hieber's bell ringers of the First Congregational Church of Battle Creek, Michigan, have constructed a special table approximately twenty feet in length and made up of folding units. A continuous upstanding music rack with lights attached also folds down flat for packing. Dr. Westcott's Spartan Ringers of Michigan State University use a similar table. Special tables have also been built in a semicircular or U-shape. Another possibility is a semicircular table top of several hinged sections which, like a banquet top, can be placed on an oblong table.

Table pads are an absolute necessity to muffle the sound of bells being set down and to protect the bells. Woolen blankets or cotton padding are useful; however, a reinforced foam-rubber pad is the best. Extra heavy padding should be arranged for broadcasting or recording sessions, as the microphone picks up thuds not heard under ordinary conditions.

For public performance an attractive corduroy, felt, or velvet cover will be needed to hide pads and blankets. Such covers should touch the floor. The name of the ringing

46

group or sponsoring organization may be cut out of felt and applied to the frontal of the cover. Swag effects, pleats, ropes and tassels, fringe, or other tasteful, decorative arrangements add a professional touch to the over-all picture. The color selected for the cover should compliment the robes or costumes of the ringers. Try these colors with stage lighting before making a final decision. You may be unpleasantly surprised.

Bell Straps or Tapes

The problem will inevitably arise for table-bound ringers when the use of a table is not appropriate, or where there is insufficient space. Ringing in a chancel during a service of worship; ringing in a processional; appearing on narrow platforms for public events; on steps, floats, or other restricted places calls for flexibility, adaptability, and sometimes last-minute adjustments.

Groups having either a small number of bells or a number of persons ringing regardless of the number of bells, have no actual need of a table. It is quite common for bell ringing groups to "string up" several bells for carrying short distances and to place extra bells on the floor while ringing. There is some danger of chipping a bell edge against a cement or marble floor; it is safer to place such bells on small pieces of cloth or to use the bell bags for that purpose.

Another method of carrying extra bells is to suspend them on a ribbon or heavy tape around the neck within easy reach of the hands. The Cape Ann Ringers, of Gloucester, Massachusetts, and the Whitechapel Ringers of the

Atchison (Kansas) High School use this method exclusively, handling the bells skillfully and unobtrusively. Each ringer of the latter group employs four bells hung at the ends of two tapes. The heavy tape used is about two inches wide and is similar to that used by bandsmen. The first tape is placed around the neck and crossed over the chest, the bells hanging at the hip on each side. The second tape is hung, stole-like, down the front of the body, the bells hanging just below the waistline. This band of twelve rings thirty-odd bells expertly without benefit of floor or table. The tapes are part of the equipment and are packed with the bells.

Music, Music Stands, and Carriers

Sheet music, notebooks, direction or assignment sheets, and batons should be kept in special folders, boxes, or brief cases. This is an important concern of the director or librarian. Extra pencils and paper should always be available. Those groups employing charts may arrange folios of heavy cardboard or purchase large, plastic, zippered brief cases, such as those used by artists and architects. The latter are available in art stores in varying sizes and prices.

Charts are generally made of standard 22" x 28" white cardboard available at art stores and stationers for about 14 cents per sheet, less in quantity. Music may be written with India ink, crayon, felt-point pen, etc. Although black is ordinarily used for notation, other colors may be used to designate dynamics, accents, octaves, a melody within the harmony, and descants. Errors may be canceled by applying a piece of white gummed paper or white mystic tape over the mistake. When a selection requires more than one page, a sheet of cardboard may be cut in half and one half taped to the center of the uncut sheet, making a page to turn. A number of half sheets may be taped to each side of one chart.

Directors using sheets of music often use colored pencils to accent notes and directions.

The use of sheet music or chart poses the problem of the holder. Although sheet music may be laid flat on the table, reading soon becomes tiresome and it is difficult to watch the director. Table racks are helpful, and two ringers may share one rack. The disadvantage of table racks is that there is the danger of striking bells against the rack and, again, some inconvenience in watching the director. Groups using standing music racks and table must stand some distance from the table. This is awkward for picking up and replacing bells on the table, and there is still the danger of hitting the rack. Music racks may be raised to varying heights and shared by two ringers.

One central chart placed on an easel in front of the ringing group solves many problems. The director may stand by the chart, conduct, turn pages, and change charts. The band or choir will make a better appearance with attention focused on the director and chart; at rehearsals the director can immediately point out a part to be rehearsed, can quickly make cuts without confusion; in the church service, a chart can be inconspicuously placed where it may be seen only by the ringers; a chart can be placed out of camera range on TV programs, only one

49

light is necessary when playing on a poorly lighted stage, in a candlelit setting, or out-of-doors at night.

A dependable easel is a necessity for those using charts. A light folding wooden or aluminum artist's easel is useful and not expensive. Test the easel for its holding ability on waxed and marble floors, as rubber and metal tips do slide with disastrous effects. Make the easel foolproof with light chains or wire struts between the legs.

A fluorescent light may be clamped to the top of an easel or to a rod extension. A light, an extension cord, and double sockets should be part of the equipment. Incidentally, ringers using music racks may require a number of lighting fixtures.

Standard equipment should include a repair kit. Time will be saved and distress allayed if the following are always on hand: spare leather or wooden pegs, small felt pieces for springs, a tube of quick-drying glue, a pair of small long-nosed pliers, mystic tape or cloth strips to bind temporarily unexpected breaks in leather handles. And most important of all, include a small can of oil. (See Chapter VII on care of handbells.)

The equipment should also include a first-aid kit. This means Band-aids or similar tape bandage. The "professional disease" or bell ringers is finger and palm blisters. Inexperienced ringers should wear gloves. Many groups have gloves as a part of their costume; others keep old gloves for use in practice sessions. The most seasoned players may suffer blisters in hot, sticky weather.

50

Costumes or Robes

The appearance of any ringing group is enhanced by attractive, colorful robes or costumes. Robes or costumes make for uniformity, add a professional touch, and build up pride and interest in the organization.

Bell choirs, wearing the vestments of the church, may be allowed to add a ribbon, insigne, or other appurtenance to the regulation robe. For nonservice appearances, such choirs enjoy a costume or at least an informal white blouse-dark skirt or pants type of matched outfit. The Cathedral Ringers of Atlanta, Georgia, besides choir robes and a troubadour costume, also sport dark bermudas, white shirts, long white socks and black shoes. *Shoes* must be uniform with all groups. One pair of off-color shoes, as well as varying lengths of robes, may ruin the appearance of the entire group. Girls and ladies should avoid spike heels and costume jewelry.

Chapter VI

Management and Policies of Handbell-Ringing Groups

Assistants

THE AVERAGE HANDBELL DIRECTOR IS A BUSY PROFESSIONAL musician. The ringing band or choir is only one of a number of groups with which he must meet every week. As he is often the music arranger and copyist as well as the director, he should be ably assisted and relieved of the other mechanics of operation by a dependable slate of officers, or, in the case of youngsters, assisting adults.

Elected officers should include a president or manager, assistant or student directors, treasurer, publicity manager, librarian, and robe or costume manager. In young people's groups, assistants might include bell choir mothers and parents available for transportation and chaperonage purposes.

The president or manager should assist the director in every possible way, represent the group when requested, oversee and check on the proper functioning of the other officers and the care and maintenance of the bells, help with discipline, and manage concert and travel details.

He should preside at brief business meetings and at periodic elections.

Assistant and student directors may be elected or chosen by the director from among experienced ringers with leadership potential and given opportunities to conduct at rehearsals and performances. Assistants may direct second-string or younger ringing groups and give special instruction to new ringers.

The treasurer should collect dues or make collections for special needs, as decided by the group, and serve as chairman of the Ways and Means Committee for money-raising projects such as the purchase of new bells, the purchase of robes or costumes, financing bell trips or tours. He will keep accounts of all the funds and make regular reports to the membership.

The publicity manager should check ideas for publicity with the director and should be responsible for sending notices to the press, local organizations and publications, radio stations, sponsors, and fans. He should keep on hand mimeographed copies of information (press releases) concerning the group and the director; printed brochures and posters, if available; sample programs, pictures, tape recordings and records. He—or an assistant—should maintain a scrapbook of press notices, programs, and pictures.

The librarian should be responsible for having the proper music or charts on hand at rehearsals, for filing it away, or for readying it for a concert; for mimeographing and helping to copy music or to make charts. He should also take care of the ringers' notebooks and instruction sheets and see that ringers are supplied with the proper information sheets and programs before concerts.

Ringing groups having robes or costumes will require the services of costume managers or bell choir mothers. Adult groups may be self-sufficient, but young people's groups will need one or more bell choir mothers or chaperones. These good angels should inspect the robes or costumes periodically, press them, or have them laundered or dry-cleaned, and make necessary repairs. Costume managers or choir mothers should accompany the ringing groups to concerts and on tours and should oversee the transportation and packing of costumes or robes.

Rules and Regulations for Ringers

REHEARSAL PROCEDURE:

A regular rehearsal schedule should be set up and, if possible, never changed. The time announced means "playing time," and all equipment should be set out in position and ready by that time, unless class hours are to be considered.

Bell choirs may wish to commence rehearsals with a prayer followed by a response, such as a hymn played on the bells; other groups may prefer to open with a patriotic selection or an alma mater.

Directors will differ about rehearsal techniques, but in general they will follow the average choral or instrumental director's procedure of briefly warming up; playing through several well-known favorite selections as a further loosening-up; tackling ticklish spots in several new selections, then sailing through the entire piece, just once, letting the chips fall where they may; further rehearsing other half-baked selections; spot-checking others that go well; calling a brief intermission for stretching, announcements, and business; then a shorter, concentrated period for precision and polish; and lastly, a favorite selection for a rousing windup.

Before the bells are put away, every ringer must polish his bells with the soft cloths that are always kept on hand with the equipment. *This is important.*

The necessary tasks of unpacking and setting up equipment for rehearsals, as well as for concerts, and repacking should be definitely assigned to certain ringers by the president or manager. He may post a list and rotate names monthly. When everyone willingly co-operates, these tasks take only a matter of minutes, and no one person is the goat. Any person who refuses to do his share should be rung out of the group.

ABSENCES:

Bell ringers must be more careful about absences and tardiness than members of almost any other organization. One absent ringer inconveniences the group, two absent members seriously cripple the group, while if there are more than two absent, the rehearsal may as well be canceled.

A ringer should notify the director as far ahead as possible if he *must* be absent. The director can then call a substitute or rearrange the rehearsal schedule. Some groups have several "roving ringers"—experienced players who can handle extra bells and who can take over in case of an absence. This practice, in itself, is often an absentee deterrent, as many ringers become slavishly devoted to "my bells"! Ringing groups develop a remarkable *esprit de corps* and absences are rare. The director should avoid ringing regularly with the ensemble.

Young people, especially, must be trained to watch the director for attacks, releases, dampening, and dynamic signals. The director may use a baton, but for small groups the hands are perhaps more intimate. These finer points may be learned only by concentrated repetition in rehearsal, week after week—the start-and-stop-and-try-again method. When rehearsal time is limited, as in a warm-up session immediately preceding a concert, it is well to "foolproof" even the best-known selections by ringing the opening chord only, or a tricky entrance or cutoff.

The experienced director keeps every ringer "in the palm of his eye" and establishes such a rapport between himself and the group that it will respond to his every mood and motion. The eyes and the expression of the director are important.

Rehearsals should move along briskly; unnecessary talking should be absolutely discouraged. Sounding bells "for fun" between selections and before and after rehearsals should be a major offense. It is discourteous to the director and the other ringers and is a dangerous mishandling of the bells.

Rules may be set up with penalties for absences, tardiness, failure to carry out assigned tasks (such as putting bells away, unnecessary disturbances, touching the metal part of the bell).

AWARDS:

Young people, especially, appreciate awards; and a definite system of suitable awards should be planned for them. Felt or embroidered emblems to be sewn on pockets or sleeves, service stripes, jewelry with bell designs, small ceramic or metal bells are all enthusiastically received. The "bell metal" pin and felt emblems, available through the American Guild of English Handbell Ringers, should be earned and presented with discretion.

POSTURE:

The director must insist on good ringing posture at all times. He may allow ringers to sit during part of a long rehearsal. Even when seated, a ringer must hold his bells up straight at chest height, and shoulders and head are erect.

Position of Bells on Tables

Ringing groups employing tables may be trained to pick up their bells with a flourish in a unison motion of precision at the beginning of a program. This is especially effective when the group wear white gloves.

Handbells may either be laid flat on a table, with the handles toward the ringer, or set upright. This is a matter for the director to decide. It may be argued at length as to the convenience and speed of picking up handles, whether prone or upright, which position is the more attractive visually. The English employ both positions. It it recommended by the manufacturer that the heaviest octave of handbells, C 29 to C 22 (Whitechapel), be kept in the horizontal position, unless extra thick padding is provided.

Procedure in Services of Worship

Ordinarily, ringing choirs do not bring tables into church for services of worship, but carry the bells in during a processional or place them on or under seats before the service. Bells carried in processional may be held upright or against the chest when not being rung. A table might be hidden in a balcony or chancel, but this can be avoided if the director will plan music requiring only the number of bells that can be carried, worn around the neck, or placed on seats.

Music may be memorized, placed on hymn racks, or on music stands; or a chart may be set up where it can easily be seen by all ringers. The director may direct from the organ bench or from some other position, preferably invisible to the congregation.

Bell choirs moving out on the chancel steps or to the head of the main aisle, with director in front, may be accused of "performing" during a service of worship.

Keeping the mechanics of operation simple and inconspicuous should be the goal of bell choirs ringing in church. The main problem is to avoid making "clinking" sounds before and after playing. A suggested remedy is to place the bells on cloth under the seat or to wrap them in cloth when not in use. As the time approaches to ring, or when the ringer has finished, he must move slowly so the clappers are still, and carefully that the bells do not touch one another or the next ringer's bells. Extraneous bell sounds are distressing to the devout worshiper, and this lack of consideration (or training) on the part of some bell choirs, as well as the director's poor taste in selecting music, has caused handbells to be considered unsuitable by some conservative churches.

All ringing to be done in church must be rehearsed in the church. The tonal effects may be vastly different from those in the rehearsal room. If the bells are to ring with organ, choir, other instruments, or in the processional, several rehearsals would be wise. To avoid confusion, seating arrangements of bell ringers must be carefully planned and rehearsed. When ringing hymns as the congregation sings, whether in procession or not, the bell choir must be absolutely self-sufficient, yet perfectly with the organ. There should be repeated rehearsals to achieve this—counting off the exact number of beats desired between stanzas and after the introduction, which stanzas are *tacet,* and when to ring a descant. This should be done well, or else not attempted. Practice hymn ringing on the Sunday school or other groups before appearing in church.

Because of the acoustical time lag in most church buildings, handbell choirs ringing in processions coming from the rear of the church had best wait and ring when in the middle or front of the church unless the organ has a rear unit.

Ideal settings for the performance of the bell choir are the rear gallery or the back of the sanctuary. With no whisper, rustle, or clink, at the appointed moment—bells ring. This might truly be an exalted spot of beauty, a ray of light in the service, and could lift hearts of the congregation in gladsome praise to the glory of God.

Concert Procedure

MECHANICS:

Ringing bands presenting programs in auditoriums or on stages or platforms should work out definite procedures and rules in order to facilitate the mechanics of the performance, to clear the way for the group to function smoothly and successfully, and to make the most attractive and professional appearance.

The director and the advance guard (president or manager, or assistants assigned to this job) should arrive early if unfamiliar with the building or setting. They should check on the following details, which also should have been discussed when the invitation for the concert was accepted: (1) arrangements for someone to be there to open up a full hour before the performance; (2) space available for performance; (3) lighting, available plugs, house lights to be up or down during program; (4) curtains— to be drawn or not, and when; (5) acceptable background; (6) stage entrances and exits; (7) dressing-room facilities; (8) chairs on stage, if desired; (9) amplification, if necessary; (10) loading entrance for groups with tables, heavy boxes, and costumes; (11) available stage crew.

Ringing bands having tables, covers, and other equipment, might well set up as far ahead as possible before the concert, especially if the platform is in open view. Bells should never be set out and left unattended. They may be locked in an office or closet until near the concert hour.

Costumes should be hung out and ready. Dressing rooms can usually be locked; if not, arrangements must be made ahead of time about valuables.

WARM-UP:

When the ensemble is completely robed or costumed, and if time permits, a warm-up is most desirable. Sometimes it is possible to arrange a rehearsal at home base before a nearby concert. If the band is not allowed to make a sound, even a "dry" or silent run is helpful to remind players of weak spots.

Stage Entrances and Positions

Entrances, exits, bows, when to sit should all be rehearsed and thoroughly understood by every member of the band. The line-up and spacing for entrances and exits is important. If a curtain is used, is the band to be in place as it rises, or to enter after? And, in reverse, does the curtain close on the ensemble or after it has filed out? The spacing and arrangement of a band in ringing position is important. Do the ringers stand in a straight line, a semicircle, or two or more staggered lines; and are heights and sex considered, or the assignment of bells? Positions for concerts should be the same as positions for rehearsals, for a ringer becomes accustomed to the sounds emanating from the neighboring ringer, and a sudden change may throw him for a loss. Groups using tables will have assigned, regular positions and this will be no problem for a public performance.

It is usually better theater for the director to take bows for the ensemble, except for individual soloists. At the conclusion of a program, the director may move to one side of the stage and make a motion toward the band while the band stands in place and smiles graciously.

Fees for Handbell Ringing

HANDBELL CHOIRS:

Should bell choirs charge for programs away from the home church? The final decision will rest, in each instance, with the church authority; and the policy should be cleared and thoroughly understood by all concerned before invitations are accepted. A number of bell choirs *do* charge a fee or accept a donation which varies for "in-town" and "out-of-town" programs. Consideration must be made of transportation, food, and other expenses. Such programs have defrayed the cost of handbells, robes or costumes, trips to bell festivals, and have aided church or music funds, or other benefits.

OTHER RINGING GROUPS:

Handbell ringers in general ring chiefly for the joy and pleasure it brings to themselves and others, and for fellowship and recreation. Every group gladly volunteers to ring programs at hospitals, "homes," and for community projects such as the lighting of the Christmas tree. Although a few ringing bands do not accept an honorarium, the majority find a fee or subsidy necessary for existence. Unless the school or sponsoring organization is not in favor of it, most bands maintain a treasury to cover their needs and do charge fees ranging from token fees of twenty-five dollars to fees of several hundred dollars.

AMPLIFICATION OF HANDBELLS:

Amplification does not help the tone quality of handbells, and there are Bell Directors who refuse to allow its use. However, when a handbell program is to be given in an unusually large or "dead" auditorium, it is fairer to use amplification than have part of the audience unable to hear at all. There should be at least two microphones, and three for larger groups. The apparatus must be carefully tested—and even adjusted during the performance if necessary. If the director is to make announcements, he deserves a separate microphone.

Ringing from Memory

Ideally, ringing from memory produces the most desirable results musically and technically. Practically, it is impossible for the average group to memorize more than a few single melodic lines and perhaps one or two selections, if that.

Most groups meet only once a week; and although adults may rehearse longer, young people's classes usually last from forty-five to fifty minutes. With the many programs bell ringers are called upon to give during a season, it is just not humanly possible to practice group memorization.

The few groups ringing programs from memory are either school or college bands made up of musicians who play several instruments and have a number of ringing rehearsals, or an occasional choir or band that has unusual opportunities for rehearsal but probably has a limited repertoire.

Almost unsurmountable handicaps in playing from memory, for any ringing group, are how to meet the situation when a ringer becomes suddenly ill and the problem of breaking in new ringers.

Handbell Recordings and Pictures

Like today's amateur photographers, few persons wishing to record a handbell program have the courtesy to ask permission of the director or manager. Ringing bands having recordings and pictures for sale may prefer not to be taped or snapped. If the band is not up to par, the director may not wish a recording of that particular performance. Unscrupulous persons have been known to copy bell arrangements from a recording.

Handbell Tapes and Records

Handbells are difficult to record satisfactorily. The bell reverberation and hum is intensified, causing the music to be blurred and distorted. Mechanical sounds of clapper blows, clicks, and thuds of bells being set down on the tables are all present in exaggeration. Even with the latest and finest hi-fi or stereo equipment, handbell records and tapes are, at best, inclined to be monotonous. Perhaps the chief attraction of handbells is in the ringing or in auditing the sweep and verve of a "live" performance.

Except for having a few tapes or records made privately for the pleasure and satisfaction of the band membership or for the study of techniques of playing and arranging music by directors, groups are cautioned about going overboard in having quantities of records pressed. It is unwise to make such an expensive investment unless returns are assured. Numerous managers of retail record shops have expressed the opinion that no bell records of any type sell in quantity.

Chapter VII

How to Arrange
and Write Music for Handbells

From dulcet tongues, the notes ring out
Their harmony spread all about,
Life's petty things to put to rout,
    The Bell Ringers! *

—AGNES CARR

LITTLE MUSIC HAS EVER BEEN WRITTEN FOR HANDBELLS.

Books and pamphlets compiled for change ringing contain only the patterns of numbers used in ringing changes. Change ringing is founded on mathematical rather than musical principles. However, the musician is more interested in tune ringing, a natural outgrowth of change ringing.

Handbell ringing is unique in that the ringing director must write or adapt the music that is played. Although a small amount of original music for handbells is now available and some carillon music is usable, a large pro-

* By permission of the Boston Herald-Traveler Corporation.

portion of a band's repertoire consists of music borrowed from other mediums and adapted to suit handbells.

Not all music is adaptable for handbells. Symphonic, operatic, and organ literature, chamber music, and involved contrapuntal music had best be avoided. Rhythmically uncomplicated hymns, spirituals, folk songs, carols, and small instrumental pieces of Bach, Mozart, Haydn, Purcell, Arne, Boccherini, and Martini lend themselves well to arrangement for handbells.

Handbells are limited as to range, volume, and technical possibilites. Repertoire must be selected to suit their peculiar qualities and intimate appeal. The arranger should keep in mind the nature of the instrument and strive for artistic effects of a high musical level within the limitations of the instrument. In other words, it is foolish to expect or to strive for pyrotechnical display or massive sound effects with handbells.

(1) Hndbell ringers should not play from piano, choral, or other music; music must be specially arranged for them. (Diagram 6.) (2) Fast tempos, rapid passages, or several notes within the beat are difficult and often impossible to ring. The larger bells are louder and resound longer than the small ones and are naturally played and sound more slowly. (3) Except for occasional staccato and chromatic effects the duration of tone is not generally controlled. (See Chapter III on dampening.) The normal characteristic of bell ringing is free reverberation—one tone melting into another. (4) Dynamics may be controlled by the ringer's stroke, but the clever arranger will take care that a melody is not overwhelmed by harmony, by limiting the

67

Diagram 6

"O Master, Let Me Walk with Thee"

Diagram 7

In 4- and 6-beat measure arrangements, one chord harmonization is often too bare and may sound amateurish.

"All Creatures of our God and King"

Diagram 8

However, double up on octaves and fill in harmony for occasional mass effects, for finales, or to accompany audience singing.

"Fairest Lord Jesus"

Diagram 9

SA and SSA arrangements are effective with small numbers of handbells.

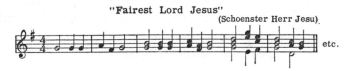

"Fairest Lord Jesus"
(Schoenster Herr Jesu)

etc.

harmony to fewer voices, or slower notes, or accompanimental figures. (Diagram 7.) (5) Bass bells, in close harmony, are surprisingly sonorous and strikingly beautiful. (6) A climax with a high melody note should be reinforced with full harmony. (7) For finales or bravura effects, double the melody, and perhaps the harmony, too, in octaves. (Diagram 8.)

Beginning groups may start out ringing only the melodies of well-known songs or hymns, the director gradually writing in the harmony. (Diagram 9.) Unison may be alternated with passages of harmony. The last verse or stanza might be rung in full harmony, or in unison octaves.

Bell arrangements are effective with the melody well articulated and the harmony fullest on strong beats, as the first measure of "Let All Mortal Flesh":

Diagram 10

"Let All Mortal Flesh"
(Picardy)

Avoid repeated, clumpy chords, unless accompanying congregational singing when all the stops must be pulled out to produce sheer volume. Don't limit the melody to the soprano line. Write the melody for the bass, or lowest, bells occasionally, or for an inner part. Here is an example with the melody written below—an arrangement of Brahms' "Lullaby" for fourteen bells:

Diagram 11

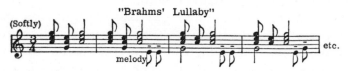

Simple melodies without big intervals or chromatics arranged with variations and modulations are good. Variations may be added as the ringing group grows in proficiency and conveniently cut or skipped during performance. (See Diagram 12.)

Simple contrapuntal writing is often more interesting than harmonic and is a welcome contrast with its flow of movement. Care should be taken not to space notes too widely, in any style, as the music becomes thin and may fall apart.

Something has to be done about ties and holds. The duration of tone of higher (smaller) bells is only a few seconds. Above 12 F (see p. 61 Whitechapel numbering), the tremulando may be employed to sustain the melody or other notes. Accents and shading are both possible with the tremulando. Carillonneurs use this device frequently, but it can be overdone and become fussy and tedious.

Trills, mordents, and grace notes are also useful ornamentations. (See Chapter IV, Tremulando and Trill.)

Arranging for the Small Ring of Bells

Arranging music for a small ring of bells presents a challenge to the most gifted and resourceful musician. It takes imagination and skill to provide a variety of interesting effects within a limited range of pitches. A

Diagram 12

Brighten familiar tunes with descants and variations. These will cut through chorus and congregational singing, and will add beauty and luster.

"O God, Our Help In Ages Past" (St. Anne)

etc.

frequent criticism of many small ringing groups is the monotony and similarity of their repertoire. Tempi, style, and material should be varied and contrasting.

Musicians arranging for small rings, particularly, should make use of light harmony under the melody, avoid inversions, and make certain the final chord is in root position or tonic unison. (Diagram 13.)

Methods of Scoring Handbell Music

There are at least three methods used for writing out handbell music: music notation, numbers, and letters.

While normal music notation is most generally accepted, number and letter systems have merit and are worthy of consideration.

Directors with small rings of bells, working with young children, the handicapped, the elderly, and perhaps meeting irregularly for rehearsal, may find numbers or the numbering of notes useful. A problem with this method is the likelihood of confusing note numbers with beat numbers. The advantages are its simplicity and the encouragement and pleasure it gives the nonmusician.

Letters are used by groups of ringers, some of whom may not read music, whose rehearsal time is limited, and who wish to ring a larger repertoire of music than would otherwise be possible to learn. This method requires the use of charts, and unless the selections are short, charts that unfold or have pages to turn. (See Chapter IV, Music and Carriers.) The lettering system is similar to music notation in that it outlines the staff, letters are written in the approximate position of notes, and the usual time signature, dynamic and expression marks, and other symbols are used.

The advantage of letters in scoring is the ease with which the inexperienced quickly learn to ring a large number of selections of some difficulty—handles of bells are marked with the pitch name. If a ringer holds an A bell, it is not difficult for him to learn to ring that bell whenever an A appears on the chart. Letters take up less space than notes and staves; therefore, many more measures can be written on one chart page. By this method ringers painlessly learn a great deal about music despite them-

Diagram 13

Arrangements for small sets of handbells should avoid first and second inversion chords at final cadences, etc.

"Were You There?" (Spiritual)

NOT

BETTER

selves, and as a result find that they are soon able to read music quite easily—that music is not, after all, a language of mystery.

ENGLISH NOTATION:

"Traditional" usages of notation by English bands vary surprisingly. Several large ringing bands use individual music scores similar to orchestral parts. Others use full music scores with notes or numbers, reading from table racks or single charts. The Whites of Appleton ring country folk music from figured bass scores. Frederick Sharpe arranges music in a modal style, and writes it out on charts using a system of numbers which shows the influence of change ringing notation. Mr. Sharpe has unearthed a footnote of historic interest: in 1658, during the Puritan Rebellion, Oliver Palmer of Bedford, an ingenious ringer, disguised bell compositions by writing the scores in Hebraic characters.

Program Building

The choice of material selected for programs should be varied as to tempo, key, color, dynamic contrast, as well as style and period. A series of slow numbers in the same tempo, or the same key, becomes deadly dull. No matter how perfect the ensemble, bell ringing lacking color and dynamic contrast and climactic spots becomes mechanical music produced by automatons.

The nature of the occasion is, of course, a main consideration in programing, whether a formal or informal concert, a program for a school, club, banquet, patriotic or religious observance.

The formal concert is often planned chronologically, according to period or composer. A first grouping might include arrangements from the classics of the seventeenth and eighteenth centuries, with perhaps a vocal or recorder solo for added interest. A second group of folk arrangements might include haunting melodies and spirited dance tunes. A final group might consist of modern music, original handbell or carillon numbers, a familiar melody such as a spiritual or other well-known American selection, and a windup number of a rousing nature. A tasteful novelty number or beloved folk tune, softly played, would be suitable encores.

Selections for bell ringing are usually shorter than those written for other mediums. Programs should not be timed for more than an hour. Generous encores will satisfy the enthusiastic audience, but an overlong program will put it to sleep.

74

A formal concert might feature an outstanding longer selection, such as the Handel *Sonata for a Musical Clock,* an ensemble number with other instruments or voices, or a demonstration of change ringing.

Audiences unfamiliar with handbell ringing appreciate a short talk or explanation by the director concerning the history and usage of handbells and the popularity and growth of this art in America. Directors who are not apt extemporaneous speakers should read from prepared notes. Such reading should be rehearsed for clarity of enunciation, voice projection, vitality, and color, and also to establish eye contact and rapport with the audience.

If the occasion, time, and space permit, the director may wish to invite especially interested audiences to come up after the performance to "inspect the bells." The public should be warned beforehand not to touch the bells. Ringers usually enjoy this personal contact and attention and are glad to demonstrate ringing techniques for interested persons.

Ringing groups are urged whenever possible to open programs with the National Anthem. It would be a gracious gesture for bands performing in other states and countries to ring the state song or national anthem of the host state or country.

Informal concerts and brief appearances planned for clubs, banquets, and other occasions should include selections of intrinsic value to give substance and balance to the lighter and popular styles. "Dessert and froth" alone have no lasting appeal. A band would do better to spend its time on attractive arrangements of enduring folk tunes and dances than on the passing hit tunes so soon forgotten.

One of the joys of handbell ringing is the intense interest and obvious delight shown by audiences everywhere. Return engagements are frequently offered. The sound of handbells has a peculiar appeal to all age groups, to the nonmusician and to the professional musician. It behooves the musician responsible for arranging music for handbells to exercise the utmost *expertise* in craftsmanship and the most discriminating taste of which he is capable in order to produce compositions and arrangements of the highest quality.

Available Music and Material for Handbells

Available publications and other sources of handbell compositions and arrangements, books, and recordings will be found listed in the back of this manual.

COPYRIGHT LAWS:

Musicians arranging or copying music for handbells are urged to check as to whether the music is copyright or rests in public domain. Unless especially arranged and copyrighted, folk tunes, most hymns, and music composed before 1903 are in public domain. In the United States a work can be copyright for twenty-eight years and renewed for another twenty-eight years. In England the copyright holds for a fifty-year period following the death of the composer or author.

Many modern composers and publishing houses are gracious about granting permission for the arranging of a work if the arrangement is not to be used by another person or group or performed for profit.

The Music Publishers Association of the United States may eventually authorize a standardized form to be furnished by publishers to musicians making requests about arrangements.

Those who have original music published and expect to draw royalties from its sale and performance are entitled to the protection of the copyright law. For information about what you *can* do under the copyright law write: *Music Publishers Association of the U. S. A.*, 516 Fifth Avenue, New York 36, New York.

Chapter VIII

Change Ringing

Aloud let Silence first Proclaimed be,
And by consent let's make it our Decree
And fix such Laws in our Society,
As being observ'd, will keep Sobriety.
Who curse or damns or in an angry mood
Quaril or strike altho he draws no blood,
Who wears a Hat or Spur, o'er-turns a Bell,
Or by unskeelful ringing mars a peal,
Let him pay Sixpence for each single crime,
To make him cautious at another time.
A Blessing let us crave on Church and King,
And now let's peaceably begin to ring.

—CORNISH RHYME, Eighteenth Century

CHANGE RINGING IS OF PASSING INTEREST ONLY TO THE average musician, since this science of ringing produces neither melody nor harmony and has little real musical significance. When a peal is being rung the indefinite, rhythmic tonal progressions are better appreciated at some distance from the Tower.

A ring of tower bells is manned by a team of ringers

standing in a circle in a ringing chamber below the belfry, each grasping a tufted rope connected to a bell. A ringer must understand and memorize various "methods" or formulas which have been calculated by mathematicians. He must possess strong arm and back muscles in order to withstand the arduous hours of hard, physical labor required. Quoting from Scott Parry's *The Story of Handbells:*

Physical strength, a mathematical brain, and a well-developed sense of timing are prerequisites for a good ringer and, if the visitor . . . is unimpressed by the mathematical jangling of bells, he will not fail to be amazed by the concentration and endurance of the men in the ringing chamber.

Groves' Dictionary of Music and Musicians defines change ringing as "Sounding a ring of bells according to every possible combination—each of which must be used once only." A peal commences with "rounds," that is, sounding the bells in regular scale from treble to tenor (the keynote). Then the bells change their order continually without repetition and eventually come "home" to the original "rounds."

There will be only a "light touch" on the subject, but no detailed explanation or discussion of methods of change ringing in this manual. Those interested in exploring this science further may refer to the list of publications on the subject elsewhere in these pages.

With two bells two changes are possible (1-2: 2-1); on four bells twenty-four changes are possible; on a peal of seven bells, 5,040; while twelve bells increases the possible combinations to 479,001,600! A peal is frequently rung on seven bells, which requires a little over three hours of steady ringing to complete. A record was set in 1767 for an eight-bell peal that required twenty-seven hours of ringing to complete.

Change ringing, as it is known today, is not practiced on less than five bells or more than twelve. Hundreds of peals are rung on six, eight, ten, or twelve bells, all bells changing position constantly. Other peals are rung on seven, nine, or eleven bells with an eighth, tenth, or twelfth bell—the tenor (keynote bell) remaining "behind" or always ringing in the last position.

Before the middle of the seventeenth century bells rang only repetitious "rounds" or "call changes," that is, either down and up the scale from treble to tenor, or several simple variations of rounds as called out by the ringing master. In 1668 Fabian Stedman of Cambridge published a historic work, *Tintinnalogia,* in which he outlined his remarkable discovery or invention of the science of change ringing. It was probably formulated *ca.* 1640. Following the lead of the Ancient Society of College Youths, founded in 1637, many other ringing guilds were organized. Men from all walks of life became dedicated ringers and competition among the teams and guilds was keen.

Change ringing is still popular and actively practiced in the British Isles. Pealing accomplishments are carefully recorded and publicized, especially through *The Ringing World,* the weekly newspaper of the Central Council of Church Bell Ringers. This organization of ringing societies and guilds was founded in 1891. Under its auspices rules for ringers, directions for the maintenance of church bells and towers, and collections of hundreds of methods and compositions are published and are available to the public. Today, it is estimated that there are more than five thousand rings of bells in towers of the "Ringing Isles," and that some fifty thousand ringers climb steep tower steps every week of the year.

It is not difficult to understand why the tower bell ringers of the seventeenth century began to employ hand-bells for the practice of changes. The ringers could sit comfortably in the same positions assigned in the ringing chambers, learn new peals, and instruct new ringers without disturbing the community. The downstroke of the handbell represents the backstroke of the tower bell. By viewing the position of each handbell, a ringer can determine which bells have rung in any given change. This is a substitute for "rope-sight," so necessary to the experienced tower bell ringer. Due to their convenience and portability, countless peals have been rung on handbells through the years.

Ringing bands interested in adding change ringing to their repertoire should bear in mind that the average audience will not be interested in this phase of ringing. Not more than a few minutes, for the purpose of demonstration and to do homage to a great tradition, should be presented on any program.

All ringing groups should have at least a rudimentary knowledge of change ringing, the historic *raison d'être* of the English handbell. And certainly, every ringer should understand the difference between change ringing and tune ringing. There are excellent and readable explanations of change ringing in *Groves' Dictionary of Music and Musicians* and the *Encyclopaedia Britannica* (1910 edition).

Directors wishing to indoctrinate their ringers gradually might use a "light touch" of a method—that is, only a few changes—to serve as a rehearsal warm-up, as a drill for precision ringing, or as an aid toward developing a strong upstroke. A nucleus of alert ringers who seem particularly interested might be enlisted to form a team within the band to explore the intricacies of change ringing. Such a team should hold separate and extra practice sessions, as change ringing is difficult to master and time-consuming.

Chapter IX

How to Order Handbells

"Hark! Now I hear them,—ding-dong bell."
—WILLIAM SHAKESPEARE

So You Want to Order Handbells?

MUSIC DIRECTORS WHO HAVE HEARD HANDBELL RINGING AND
are inspired by the vision of successful ringing bands or
choirs in their schools or churches sometimes experience
difficulty in selling the idea to the powers that be. In such
cases suggested procedure might be to invite a ringing band
to give a demonstration concert in your town, school, or
church; or to arrange for a committee to visit the nearest
ringing band at a rehearsal or concert; or to play recordings and show pictures with explanations of bell ringing to
a committee. Concerning the initial cost, a strong talking
point is the fact that a medium-sized set of handbells is
not so expensive as a good secondhand piano.

Many directors find it advisable to own their own bells,
or an auxiliary set, so that in case of transfer or change
of position they will still have bells on hand. Also, several

83

directors have been dismayed and inconvenienced by the restrictions placed on the use of the handbells by short-sighted and unco-operative authorities. To give a few— the bells may not be taken out of the building, or the city, or the bells may be used by other organizations. There are many advantages in private ownership. Hand-bells, like diamonds and antiques, are good investments. With the present shortage handbells can be sold in a matter of hours. One outstanding bell owner is Mrs. Earl Lowder of Bellaire, Texas, who is an elementary school teacher and also youth choir director of a large church. Mrs. Lowder carries her bells from school to church at will; she also directs a bell choir for handicapped children.

Directors who work with younger groups in schools and churches and who have handbells on order might prepare the way by getting together all kinds of "bell" material— stories, pictures, plays; by starting a "bell-board"; by buy-ing a set of plastic bells or putting water in glasses or bottles and rehearsing music with bell and chime effects; by acquiring bell recordings; by arranging a visit to a nearby bell or carillon tower; by inviting a handbell group to come and ring a "benefit" program or service; by starting a project on the story of famous bells in the state or nation.

Advice to wishful handbell directors: a set of handbells *is* within the realm of possibility for you, no matter how small your school or church or how limited your means. Many directors start with a small ring of bells and add to the set gradually. There are many money-making ways, means, and schemes. Just decide you will have this, then *do it!* Interest the P.T.A., the women's associations or civic groups; or inspire your youngsters—they will do it for you! Consider interesting someone in giving bells as a memorial. Or mortgage the car and buy them yourself. Plan a Christmas surprise for next year that will thrill your students and friends and become a cherished tradition in your community. You will be repaid with joy and pleasure a hundredfold.

Principal Manufacturers of Handbells

The two main sources of handbells are the Whitechapel Foundry (Mears & Stainbank), 32-34 Whitechapel Road, London E-1, England, and Petit & Fritsen of Aarle-Rixtel, Holland (U.S.A. address: P. O. Box 427, Evanston, Illinois).

Bell manufacturers employ a numbering system (see p. 86) to indicate the pitch of each bell. Unfortunately, the two major founders use reverse numbering, which is confusing both to prospective purchasers and for conversational and correspondence purposes among directors and ringers. The numbering system should be standardized.

Diagram 14

BELL NUMBERING

"MIDDLE C"	"MIDDLE C"
(For writing and ordering)	(Actual sound)
WHITECHAPEL—C No. 15	WHITECHAPEL—C No. 22
PETIT & FRITSEN—C No. 25	PETIT & FRITSEN—C No. 13

Persons ordering bells from other firms should check concerning the numbering system used, to avoid making inconvenient mistakes.

Bell manufacturers consider all accidentals as sharps (#). Pitch names are stamped on both sides of the leather handles. If requested, the founders will stamp A-sharp on one side and B-flat on the other.

The Whitechapel Foundry Numbering System

Middle C (Whitechapel) is numbered 15 C; C-sharp as 15 C-sharp. B-flat is A-sharp, E-flat is D-sharp, and so on.

The five chromatic octaves manufactured by the Whitechapel Foundry are numbered from the bell of the lowest pitch—29 C (two octaves below middle C) through high C, which is numbered 1 C, to an octave above or 01 C. The highest octave is numbered 1 C, 1 C-sharp, 07 D, 07 D-sharp, 06 E, 05 F, 05 F-sharp, 04 G, 04 G-sharp, 03 A, 03 A-sharp, 02 B, and 01 C.

Petit & Fritsen Foundry Numbering System

Petit & Fritsen bells are numbered in reverse, as follows:

Middle C is 25 C. The lowest C, two octaves below middle C, and the equivalent of Whitechapel's 29 C, is 1 C. The octave above is 13 C, middle C is 25 C, the octave above middle C is 37 C, and high C is 49 C. Petit & Fritsen, as of 1960, does not manufacture the fifth, or highest, octave. If and when it does, the numbers would undoubtedly run from 49 C to 61 C.

The brochures of the two foundries are self-explanatory. The prospective purchaser is reminded that middle C

(Whitechapel) is 15 C, that middle C (Petit & Fritsen) is 25 C. Underline middle C with a red pencil!

Prospective handbell purchasers are urged to hear all available makes and sets of varying numbers and weights of bells before placing orders.

Pros and Cons

Whitechapel bells are characterized by the superb craftsmanship for which the British are famous, and are still tuned by hand. This foundry has cast bells continuously since 1570 and has made sets of handbells since 1700. The bell tone is silvery and mellow; the appearance is brilliant, highly burnished. Because of the necessarily slower hand production, this foundry has a waiting list and is unable to promise delivery before twenty months. No deposit is required.

The Petit & Fritsen Foundry, also an old firm, has manufactured the English-type handbell only since 1955. The Dutch-made bells are nicely outfitted and disassemble easily. These bells are tuned electronically. Bell orders are consummated within a few months. A 50 per cent deposit is required with the order. This Foundry also manufactures bell carrying cases, which are sold separately.

Other Manufacturers

Within the past few years several American firms and individuals have experimented with the production of the English-type handbell. The following are now actively manufacturing sets of American-made bells: Benard Mason of California—"Tru-Sonic Bells"; David Workman of

Kansas—"Bells of David"; and Del Roper of California—
"Golden Bells."

Handbells are still in use—and occasionally available
for purchase—that were manufactured by founders who
have discontinued producing these small bells. Such
founders include: John Taylor & Co. and Gillett & John-
son of England, and the Mayland and Deagan firms of
the United States.

Tariff on Handbells

Representatives of the Bureau of Customs of the U. S.
Government have been inconsistent about the tariff on
handbells. There are conflicting reports. The rates average
18 per cent or 19 per cent duty for any number of bells,
although some have come through duty free. The American
Guild of English Handbell Ringers is working with several
members of Congress toward legislation for duty-free ad-
mission of Handbells ordered by religious, educational,
and civic groups.

Small orders of bells and single bells may be sent parcel
post upon request; this is convenient and desirable.
Heavier sets are shipped in wooden boxes by ship and
railway express. The purchaser is advised to insist that
boxes of bells be marked for importation to the nearest
U. S. Customs Office, or a brokerage fee for handling at
the port of entry will be added to the bill; also, there may
be irritating delays.

Buying Old Bells

Buyers are advised to be careful about purchasing old
bells with which they are not familiar: (1) Check the

pitch. It may not be Standard pitch (A-440), but International (A-435), or otherwise tuned. Bells so tuned cannot be played with present-day bells or with modern instruments. (2) Consider that replacements or additions would be difficult because of uncertain pitch or structural deviations. (3) Test the tone quality. Does it have pleasing overtones? A bell may be tested for overtones by ringing the bell, then quickly touching the lip (edge) lightly. This action will dampen the strike tone, while the overtone, if any, will continue to sound. (4) Test for uniformity of tone quality. Many old bells are harsh, discordant, and hardly on speaking terms with one another. Try a chord.

The Advantages of Owning More Than One Set

Schools and churches having one or more exceedingly active ringing groups would benefit by owning a second set. Durable as are handbells, constant and hard use causes the leather handles and pegs to wear and looseness to develop in the clapper fittings. While these parts can be repaired or replaced, an auxiliary set is a great convenience, a safety measure, a teaching aid, allows additional ringing effects, and is an all-around ace in the hole.

CONVENIENCE:

Where several groups are involved duplicate bells would obviously simplify rehearsals, transportation, packing up, and general discipline.

Duplicates would solve the problem of switching bells between, and even during, selections. Long waits between selections sometimes result when many bells must change position among players.

The story has been handed down that the famous bell-ringing teams of the early nineteenth century in Lancashire, England, used as many as two hundred bells per team, employing older bells for practice and newer bells for public appearances and contests.

SAFETY:

Every bell director and ringer fears the possibility of a dropped or cracked bell. A cracked bell is not reparable, and although attempts have been made at soldering, the results are seldom satisfactory. A replacement must be ordered. The metal of a damaged bell can be melted down by the foundry; however, this necessitates packing and shipping overseas and passing through the customs officials of two countries. The slight saving is not worth the trouble. When a bell is cracked, either discard it or keep it as a horrible example.

A number of ringing groups have known the consternation caused by a cracked or lost bell, the inconvenience in rehearsal and performance of playing around the missing note, and the wait for the replacement bell. An available duplicate set can be a morale saver.

TEACHING AID AND ADDITIONAL RINGING EFFECTS:

If time is at a premium with two sets available, the director with some assistance can hold simultaneous rehearsals in different rooms. Duos, antiphonal, and echo effects can be rehearsed separately, then together during the same rehearsal period.

This author has found that duplicates provide an excellent short cut in learning ringing techniques. By placing the student ringer next to a seasoned ringer with each holding bells of the same pitches, the new ringer will immediately imitate the motions and techniques of the more experienced person and will progress rapidly.

If for some reason a weak ringer must be used in a group, especially on lower bells, a second ringer playing duplicate bells even though weak, too, would bolster the part. Each would benefit.

Elementary school music teachers with advanced ideas foresee the eventual use of handbells with large groups or classes of children in the music program, and the development of handbell orchestras and bands using many duplicate bells.

> The proof of the pudding is in the "Eating"!
> The proof of a drum is in the "Beating"!
> The proof of a song is in the "Singing"!
> So! The proof of a bell is in the "Ringing"!
> —MARGHARITTA NARAMORE

Chapter X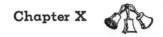

How to Care for Handbells

"Golden bells!
What a world of happiness their harmony foretells."

—EDGAR ALLAN POE

Metal

NEW HANDBELLS ARRIVE FROM THE FOUNDRY HIGHLY
burnished and it is possible and desirable to keep them
so. A ringing band or choir should take pride in the appearance and shining beauty of its bells. Dirty, tarnished
bells are unsightly.

The periodic polishing and buffing of bell metal is as
important and necessary as rubbing table silver or brass,
copper, and pewter utensils, fixtures, and ornaments. Bell
metal is a hard alloy.

Handbell directors must warn ringers and other interested persons not to touch the metal part of the bell.
Perspiration from fingers almost immediately dulls and
stains the metal. Bells may be dampened or muted against
the chest or sleeve. A number of directors insist on the use
of gloves at all times; many have strict requirements about

92

ringers polishing bells after rehearsals and before and after performances. Several times a year, or as needed, bells should be given a thorough cleaning and polish with a good cream metal polish. About once a year, buff with an electric buffer attachment, using lamb's wool and jewelers' rouge, and the bells will miraculously emerge as brilliant as when they first arrived. Wrapping bells in cloth, in cloth or plastic bags, or similar materials and storing them in a tight box or carrier is a tarnish deterrent. Bells may be shellacked successfully by brush or spray.

It is the mistaken belief of some persons that polishing a bell may alter its pitch. Representatives from both the Whitechapel and Petit & Fritsen bell foundries have stated in public and in writing that there is no harm whatsoever in polishing and buffing handbells. Scott Parry stated in *The Story of Handbells:* "If the bells have been allowed to become tarnished, they may be restored to a natural polish by buffing with a fine-grade abrasive, preferably jewelers' rouge . . . this will not alter the pitch of the bells noticeably."

Leather

Do not attempt to soften new, stiff leather handles with repeated doses of a leather dressing. Handles become pliable with use, and too supple with constant use. It is better to wear gloves or even wrap new handles with tape or cloth for a while. An occasional treatment with saddle soap will delay the tendency to crack. Handles are not difficult to replace yourself. Purchase a heavy piece of

93

leather from a wholesale leather supply company—the average shoe sole leather is too thin and pliable—mark the pattern, measuring from the old handle, cut with a sharp knife, soak briefly in hot water, then bend. Make two holes with a punch for the rivet or screw. On a Whitechapel bell the rivet holding the old handle can be removed with a drill and replaced temporarily with a nut and bolt. A machinist or someone having a rivet gun can replace the rivet. Petit & Fritsen bell handles are attached with a large screw and are thus more easily removed and replaced than those having rivets.

After constant use, or abuse, handles may become unmanageably flexible. If the leather is not cracked, rather than replace the handle, it may be stiffened or strengthened by sewing a leather strip of the same width and of several inches' length *Inside* the handle between the two strips and well below the curve, so as to have three plies together. A shoe-repair man will stitch or nail the reinforcing piece to the handle, or it may be glued or riveted.

The two leather pegs, or strikers, on the clapper are hammered in from each side. If one loosens hammer or force it back in. If a peg is lost cut another. Pegs eventually wear down and have to be replaced. Wooden pegs of small bells may be whittled from a dowel rod. These may be found at most hardware stores.

The round leather handguard or cap should last for generations unless damaged by some freak accident. Here, as with the handles, an occasional treatment with saddle soap will delay the tendency to crack with age.

94

Clapper

The clappers of handbells are detachable, thus facilitating replacement and repair. Clapper staples are either threaded and screwed into the crown of a bell, or bolted through the head or attached in similar ways. Two springs are attached to the staple, which serve as brakes for the clapper shaft, and each spring has a small piece of heavy felt glued on the inner side at the point of contact with the clapper shaft. These pieces of felt may become hard-packed and may be "pricked" as a piano tuner pricks hammer felts. If a spring felt wears thin or is lost or loose, it is simple to cut another and glue. Handbells manufactured by the Petit & Fritsen firm have pieces of felt glued on to the leather strikers to soften the tone. These are easily replaced. The lowest octave-and-a-half of bells manufactured by the Whitechapel Foundry have a strip of felt tied around the entire clapper ball and leather pegs. These felts may need replacing over a period of years. Only rarely will the felt washer, used to insulate the type of clapper staple that screws into the crown, need replacing.

Lubrication

Besides polishing the metal and storage the only care normally needed for a handbell is the occasional oiling of the clapper hinge or pivot. When a bell becomes noisy or rattles or the clapper binds, the clapper needs oiling. It will let you know! A thin oil such as neat's foot is recommended. With a small water-color brush, cotton swab, or pipe cleaner, dab a small drop of oil on the clapper hinge, carefully avoiding the felts, and work the clapper gently back and forth. The tendency is to over-oil. An excellent oiling tool is the small hypodermic-needle-like implement used for the lubrication of delicate machinery.

After long usage a clapper hinge or pin may develop a looseness, or play, and make a rattling sound. The fitting can often be tightened or the pin replaced by a machinist.

The foundries are prompt and helpful about supplying replacement clappers and other parts at small cost. Such parts are usually admitted free of duty.

Carriers

Handbell owners should be ever mindful of the safety as well as the appearance and maintenance of their instruments. It is unwise to allow children and curious adults to handle bells indiscriminately. Bells should never be tapped with metal objects or sticks, nor should they be set down on hard surfaces. During rehearsals and performances, the heaviest octave of bells manufactured—C 29 to C 22 (Whitechapel)—should be laid down when not in use, as the weight of the bell may spring the clapper fitting. Bells should be wrapped in cloth or other protective material and stored in tight boxes or carriers. Individual flannel or pacific-cloth bags and layers of foam rubber may be used for protection. (See Chapter V on carriers.)

With care, these valuable musical instruments will give good service and pleasure for many years. Remember the difficulty and expense of procuring a set, the inconvenience caused by the damage or loss of even one bell, and treat handbells with the respect and concern you would have for fragile, heirloom china.

Bibliography

A. GENERAL RESOURCES

Batty, R. E. *Church Bells*. 1850.

Brand, John. *Observations on Popular Antiquities*. 1839.

Coleman, Satis N. *Bells: Their History, Legends, Making, and Uses*. Chicago: Rand McNally & Company, 1928.

Cowlin, F. M. "Legends of Ancient Bells," *Etude*, June, 1953.

Deveson & Wace. "The Pealing of Bells," *Reader's Digest*, January, 1959.

Erb, Bessie P. "The 25th Hour," *Overtones*, Vol. 5, No. 2, 1959.

Flanders, Florence. "A New Use for Handbells," *Overtones*, Vol. 1, No. 3, 1955.

Gatty, A. *The Bell, Its Origin, History, and Uses*. 1847.

Graves, Norma R. "Bells from Across the Seas," *Etude*, August, 1954.

Haweis, H. R. "Bells and Belfries" (Eng. Illus. Mag. 1890).

Hempstead, Elliot. "I Heard the Bells," *Etude*, December, 1955.

Hone, W. *Everyday Book*. 1831-2.

Horwood, Marion. "Handbells—Ancient Art Revived," *Etude*, December, 1949.

Ingram, Thomas. *Bells in England*. London: Muller Ltd., 1954.

Knight, George Litch. *The Bells of Christmas*. (From The Bulletin, Woman's Club of Ridgewood, N. J., 1953.)

Knight, George Litch. "Handbells and Hymn Tunes," *The Hymn*, 1956.

Lawson, James T. *Societas Campanariorum* publications, 1955-60. U. of Chicago; 1960-61—Riverside Church, New York City.

Morris, Ernest. *Bells of All Nations*. London: Robert Hale, Ltd., 1951.

Morris, Governour. *Bells—Their History and Romance*. 1932.

Notes and Queries. 1859-62.

Parry, Scott B. "Casting and Tuning," *Overtones*, Vol. 1, No. 2, 1955.

Parry, Scott B. *The Story of Handbells*. Boston: Whittemore Associates, Inc., 1957.

Putnam, Mabel R. "The Singing Towers of North America," *Etude*, March, 1952.

Raven, J. J. *The Bells of England*. 1906.

Rigby, F. F. *Elementary Change Ringing*. London: S.P.C.K., 1946.

Rodgers, John. "Who? Me?" *Overtones*, Vol. 4, No. 5, 1958.

Runkle, Helen. "Pro the Small Ring," *Overtones*, Vol. 4, No. 1, 1958.

Sharpe, Frederick. *The Church Bells of Oxfordshire*. 1949-53.

Shurcliff, Margaret H. *English Bells*. 1959.

Taylor, Gladys. *Oranges and Lemons*. London: Peter Nevill, Ltd., 1954.

Walker, Stanley. "Bells," *Good Housekeeping*, September, 1945.

Walters, H. B. "Church Bells of England." Oxford Press, 1912.

Westcott, Wendell. "Handbell Arranging," "Overtones," Vol. 1, No. 4, 1955.

B. SUGGESTED MUSIC FOR HANDBELLS

1. Handbells and Organ

(Handbells may be used effectively in place of chimes; may be written in *ad lib* as introductions, interludes, imitative passages; may be used as the solo melody in choral preludes, hymn tune arrangements. Handbells are delightful in combination with other instruments such as piano, flute, recorder, and harp.)

**Andrews	Joyous Changes on Three Carols J. FISCHER
Arcadelt-Liszt-Dickinson	Angelic Salutation H. W. GRAY
Clokey	Cathedral Prelude J. FISCHER
**Couper	Pastorale (Duo for handbells and organ) J. FISCHER
Edmundson	An Easter Spring Song J. FISCHER
Gaul	Little Bells of Our Lady J. FISCHER

**Hovdesven	Three Bell Preludes
	J. FISCHER
MacFarlane	Evening Bells and Cradle Song
	SUMMY-BIRCHARD
Marryott	Carols for the Christ Child
	G. SCHIRMER
**Porter	Church Beneath the Sea
	J. FISCHER
Purcell	Bell Symphony
	NOVELLO
Roberts	Carillon
	H. W. GRAY
**Russell	Bells of St. Anne de Beaupré
	J. FISCHER
Weaver	Bell Benedictus
	GALAXY
Wesley	Holsworthy Church Bells
	H. W. GRAY
Wheeldon	The Minster Bells
	H. W. GRAY
Yon	Gesu Bambino
	J. FISCHER

2. Handbells and Choir

(Handbells are effective with vocal music. Anthems, solos, and hymn singing may be embellished with handbell accompaniment, or introduction, interludes, descants, *ad lib.*
Christmas Anthems

**Couper	Let the Merry Church Bells (SA)
	J. FISCHER
Davis, K. K.	Ding-Dong! Merrily on High (SATB, SA)
	G. SCHIRMER
**Giasson	Yule Log Carol (SATB)
	GALLEON
Holst	Christmas Song *(Personent Hodie)* (Unison)
	OXFORD PRESS

**Published with special reference to the use of handbells.

Kountz	Carol of the Christmas Chimes (All arr.)
	GALAXY
Kountz	Carol of the Sheep Bells (All arr.)
	GALAXY
**La Montaine	Nativity Morn (SATB)
	H. W. GRAY
Lockwood	Lightly, Lightly, Bells Are Pealing (SA)
	H. W. GRAY
Rawls	Christmas Bells (or Ding-Dong) (U)
	J. FISCHER
**Reinecke-Dickinson	Ring, Christmas Bells! (SA or U)
	H. W. GRAY
Wiant	A Chinese Christmas Carol (SATB or U)
	H. W. GRAY
Wood	Ding-Dong! Merrily on High (SATB, SSA, SA) E. C. SCHIRMER
Yon	Gesu Bambino (SATB or U)
	J. FISCHER

Easter and Spring Anthems

Davies	Easter Bell Carol (SA)
	FLAMMER
**Rawls	Bells of Spring (SA or U)
	J. FISCHER
Robson	An Awakening (U)
	NOVELLO
Thiman	A Song of Praise (U)
	A. P. SCHMIDT
Warner	Alleluia! To the Triune Majesty (SA)
	SUMMY-BIRCHARD

General Anthems

Bach	Jesu, Joy of Man's Desiring (SATB or U) VARIOUS
Bach	Now Thank We All Our God (SATB) E. C. SCHIRMER
Davis	Let All Things Now Living (SA or U) E. C. SCHIRMER

**Composed with handbell part.

100

Dickinson	List to the Lark (SATB)
	H. W. GRAY
Holst	A Festival Chime (St. Denio)
	(SATB or U) STAINER & BELL
Rocke	Praise Be to the God of Love—Gray
	(SATB)
Stainer	Sabbath Bells (Unison)
	H. W. GRAY
Williams, R. Vaughan	Old Hundredth (SATB)
	OXFORD PRESS

3. Handbells Alone

Carillon Music, available from the Societas Campanariorum, River-side Church, N.Y.C., is adaptable for larger sets of handbells. Write for free list. Music reasonable.

Handel, G. F. *Sonata for a Musical Clock.* Oxford Press. (Adaptable for thirteen bells—C to A.)

Litterst, R. W. *Four Pieces for Handbells.* Choral Services. (G to G —two-octave set.)

Nelson, C. Mabel. *Handbell Tutor in Staff Notation.* Jos. Williams, Ltd. (Boston Music Company.)

Runkle, Helen M. *A Handbell Concert.* J. Fischer. (A collection of twenty-three hymns, carols, folk songs, and others, arranged for a small ring of bells from middle C up.)

Stephens, Norris L. (arr.) *Christmas Music for Handbell Choirs.* (A collection of 51 carols.) Published by G. Schirmer, Inc.

Watson, Doris (arr.) . *Book of Handbell Music.* H. W. Gray, Vol. 1.

Whittlesey, Dr. F. L. (arr.) *Ringing and Singing.* (A collection of 23 hymns & carols.) Published by Flammer.

The Following Music May Be
Procured by Writing the Composers

Couper, Alinda B., 68 Allen Street, Dobbs Ferry, New York. (Music original and arranged for sets of thirteen, twenty-five, and thirty-seven bells. Watch Flammer & J. Fischer for Couper publications.)

Fay, Frederic L., 55 Park Street, West Lynn, Massachusetts. (Music original and arranged for sets of twelve, two octaves, and two-plus.)

Johe, Edward, First Congregational Church, Columbus 15, Ohio. (Music original and arranged; also with organ and flute.)

Litterst, Richard W. (Music arranged for two-octave sets—G to G. Also publication.) Second Congregational Church, Rockford, Illinois.

Tufts, Nancy Poore. Write Societas Campanariorum, Riverside Church, New York City. (Ten arrangements for ten to fourteen bells. Also arrangements for two-octave sets—G to G.)

Westcott, Wendell, Michigan State University, East Lansing, Michigan. (Arrangements for large sets of bells.)

Whittlesey, Federal Lee, Highland Park Methodist Church, Dallas, Texas. (Eight arrangements for two-octave sets—G to G.)

Available Handbell Recordings

Berkshire Ringers — (12″) Audio Fidelity

Cathedral Bell Ringers — Whittemore Associates, Inc., Boston, Massachusetts

Congregational Church Ringers — First Congregational Church, Battle Creek, Michigan

Pilgrim Bell Choir — First Congregational Church, Columbus, Ohio

Rock Creek Church Ringers (also Norbury Ringers of England and Potomac English Handbell Ringers of Washington, D. C.) — Write Nancy Poore Tufts, 9051 River View, S.E., Washington 22, D.C.

Available Books

Parry, *The Story of Handbells.* Whittemore Associates, Inc.
Watson, *The Handbell Choir.* H. W. Gray.

Other Publications

Overtones—Official Publication of the American Guild of English Handbell Ringers, Box 3141, Washington 10, D.C.

The Ringing World—Official Journal of the Central Council of Church Bell Ringers of England, c/o Woodbridge Press, Ltd., Guildford, Surrey, England.

Robes and Costumes

Bell Ringers' Robes—E. R. Moore Co., 932 Dakin St., Chicago 13, Illinois.

C. A BIBLIOGRAPHY OF BOOKS AND PAMPHLETS ON CHANGE RINGING

Instructions and Diagrams for Beginners. "The Times" Printing Works, Northgate, Blackburn, England: Lancashire Association of Change Ringers.

The Jasper Snowdon Change Ringing Series. Write Mrs. Winifred Turner, 73 Braithwaite Gardens, Stanmore, Middlesex.
  1. Rope-Sight
  2. Standard Methods
  3. Surprise Methods
  4. Grandsire

Powell, E. S. M. *The Ringer's Handbook.* London: W. & G. Foyle, London WC 2, England, or Mrs. E. S. Powell, Wellington, Somerset.

Publications of the Central Council of Church Bell Ringers. Write The Editor, c/o Woodbridge Press, Ltd., Guildford, Surrey.
  1. Central Council Handbook
  2. Beginners' Handbook
  3. Preservation and Repair of Bells (Tower Bells)
  4. Collection of Plain Major Methods
  5. Change Ringing on Handbells
  6. Methods Sheets
  7. Collections of Peals
  8. On Conducting
  9. *Village Bells* (by R. Howes—new edition)
  10. Instructions on Care of Church Bells (Card)
  11. Model Code of Rules, and other publications

Rigby, F. F. *Elementary Change Ringing.* London: SPCK, 1956. (Write SPCK, 69 Great Peter St., London S.W. 1, England.)

Troyte, C. A. W. *Change Ringing.* London, 1869. (Out of print.)

N.B.—Change Ringing is extremely difficult and complicated. *Village Bells,* the Central Council's *Beginners' Handbook,* and Rigby's *Elementary Change Ringing* are suggested for the beginner.

Also Good Reference Reading

"Bells"—Change Ringing. *Encyclopaedia Britannica* (1910 ed.).

"Change Ringing." *Groves' Dictionary of Music.* New York: The Macmillan Company, 1935. I, 601-2.

Morris, Ernest. *The History and Art of Change Ringing.* London: Chapman & Hale, Ltd., 1931.

Nichols, John R. *Bells Through the Ages.* (London, 1928.)

Sayers, Dorothy. *The Nine Tailors.* New York: Harcourt, Brace & Company, 1934. (A detective novel of interest to change ringers.)

Index

107

Date Due

Demco 293-5